ONE-BOARD
WOODWORKING
PROJECTS

ONE-BOARD
WOODWORKING
PROJECTS

ANDY STANDING

The Taunton Press

The Taunton Press
Inspiration for hands-on living®

The Taunton Press, Inc., 63 South Main Street
P.O. Box 5506, Newtown, CT 06470-5506
e-mail: tp@taunton.com
All rights reserved

First published 2012 by Guild of Master Craftsman Publications Ltd
Castle Place, 166 High Street, Lewes, East Sussex BN7 1XU

Text © Andy Standing, 2012
Copyright in the Work © GMC Publications Ltd, 2012

Library of Congress Cataloging-in-Publication Data

Standing, Andy.
  One-board woodworking projects : woodworking from the scrap pile / Andy Standing.
    p. cm.
  Summary: "This book is a clearly illustrated, practical guide to building fabulously functional household projects from a single plank of wood"-- Provided by publisher.
  ISBN 978-1-60085-779-9 (pbk.)
  1. Woodwork--Amateurs' manuals. I. Title.
  TT185.S685 2012
  684'.08--dc23
                          2012008138

The publishers and author can accept no legal responsibility for any consequences arising from the application of information, advice or instructions given in this publication.

Publisher: Jonathan Bailey
Production Manager: Jim Bulley
Managing Editor: Gerrie Purcell
Senior Project Editor: Wendy McAngus
Editor: Simon Smith
Managing Art Editor: Gilda Pacitti
Designer: Robert Janes
Photography: Anthony Bailey and Andy Standing
Illustrator: Simon Rodway

Set in ITC Avant Garde Gothic
Color origination by GMC Reprographics; Printed and bound in China by Hung Hing Printing Co Ltd
10 9 8 7 6 5 4 3 2 1

About Your Safety

Working wood is inherently dangerous. Using hand or power tools improperly or ignoring safety practices can lead to permanent injury or even death. Don't try to perform operations you learn about here (or elsewhere) unless you're certain they are safe for you. If something about an operation doesn't feel right, don't do it. Enjoy the craft, but keep safety foremost in your mind whenever you're in the shop.

FOREWORD

Making and creating things is a wonderful way to satisfy the creative urge that is innate in most of us. Producing items for your home and garden is also a great way to express yourself and personalize your living space.

Woodworking is one such way of making things you can be proud of, and you need only a basic tool kit and a few accessories to be able to do some wonderful work. Of course, most of us do some DIY, repairing and fitting things, but you can use your existing tools to help you make individualized projects for specific areas.

This book shows how to make 20 such projects in easy-to-follow steps that will help build your confidence as well as show the basics of construction that underpin making any such project.

Just be warned! Woodworking is fun and if, like me, you catch the woodworking bug, then you will no doubt go on to make many more items for friends and family. Have fun!

Mark Baker
Editor, Woodturning & Woodcarving *magazines*

CONTENTS

The Projects

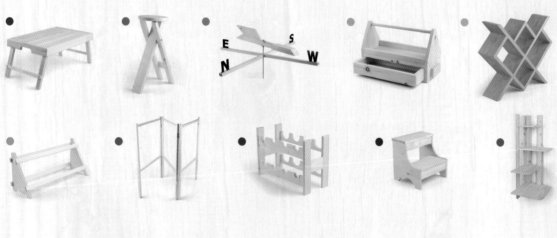

INTRODUCTION

So what can you make with one board? A floorboard, perhaps, or a shelf?
Well, with a bit of imagination, there is a lot more that you can do.

The aim of this book is to provide you with some plans and inspiration to construct a range of useful and functional items for the home and workshop, but without the need for complicated lists of materials. All are made using prepared boards, which can easily be obtained from a local lumberyard or home center.

Each project can be made from a single board, with the occasional need for some hardware such as bolts or hinges, and perhaps the odd piece of sheet material such as plywood.

Construction techniques are straightforward, mixing both traditional wood joinery with more modern methods. The projects can all be made using hand tools alone, though using power tools will obviously speed things up a bit.

Many of the projects may also be modified to suit your particular needs. Don't feel that you must stick to the published dimensions. You might want a plate rack with more spaces, or a bigger rocking chair. If so, simply scale up the plan as you like. It is important not only to make what you want, but also to enjoy the experience. Perhaps it will inspire you to start designing and making your own projects.

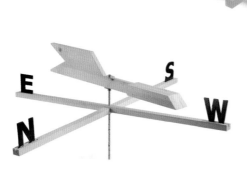

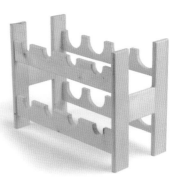

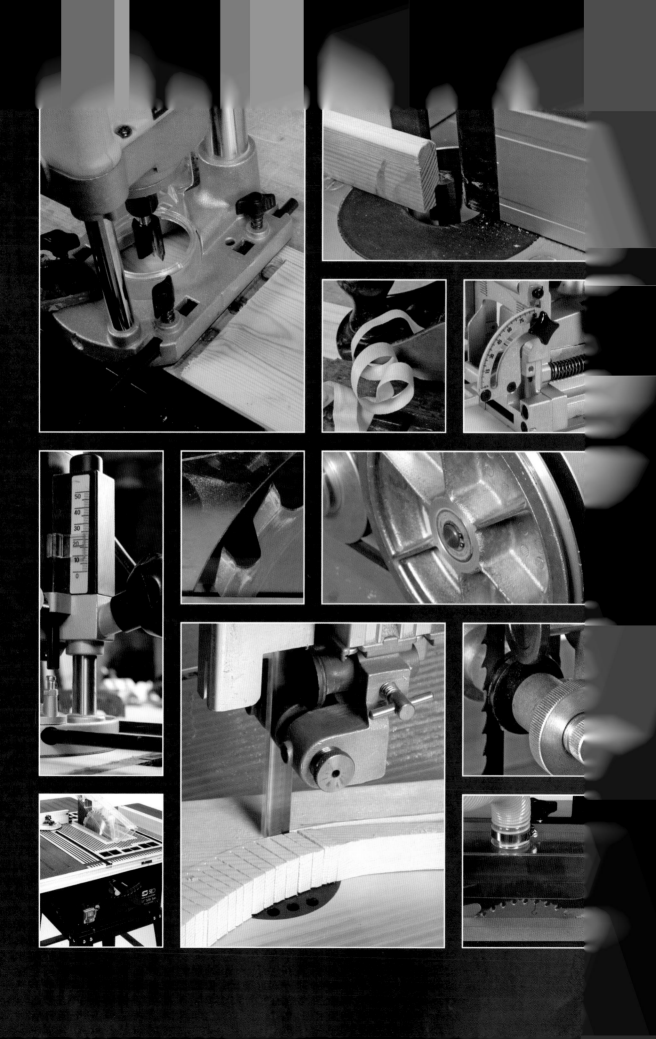

BASICS

CHAPTER ONE

TOOLS AND EQUIPMENT

Successful woodworking relies on many factors, and one of the most important is your tool kit. To complete any project, you will need a range of tools. Whenever you buy any, always choose the best that you can afford. Good-quality tools are expensive, but the money is never wasted. They will give you years of service if properly cared for, and their superior quality will make them easier to use. Cheap tools are invariably a false economy. They will be poorly designed and made from inferior materials, resulting in poor performance and disappointing results.

A well-equipped workshop will house a range of hand tools, power tools, and possibly a few machines. It can all seem a bit daunting for the novice woodworker, however, so here is a guide to a range of tools that you can use to make the projects in this book.

HAND TOOLS

You will need a small selection of hand tools as well as measuring and marking instruments.

MEASURING AND MARKING

For general measuring, use a flexible steel tape or a steel rule. A try square and a combination square are useful for marking out, and a protractor and sliding bevel are needed for marking angles. A compass is also useful, as is an inexhaustible supply of pencils.

Tools for measuring and marking

SAWS

A selection of saws is useful. A saw with hardened teeth can be used for both ripping and crosscutting. For finer crosscutting, use a tenon saw—although you may prefer a pull saw, which, as the name suggests, cuts on the pull stroke. This means that it does not need stiff blades and can have a thin, flexible blade with razor-sharp Japanese-style teeth that cut a thin kerf with great accuracy.

These saws are all designed to cut in a straight line. For making curved cuts, use a coping saw. This has a metal frame with a narrow blade stretched across it. The orientation of the blade can be adjusted in the frame, so that the saw can cut in any direction. The blades are fragile and easily broken, but they are cheap to replace.

Selection of saws

PLANES

Once you have sawn your lumber, you need to smooth the edges and correct any problems. A plane is the tool for this. Planes are made in a bewildering array of styles and sizes, from immense jointer planes through to tiny shoulder planes. To get started, however, you only really need two: a smoothing plane and a block plane.

Smoothing and block planes

CHISELS

You will find a small set of chisels extremely useful. A well-sharpened chisel is a versatile tool capable of a range of functions, from cutting joints to shaping details. Choose bevel-edged examples.

HAMMERS AND MALLETS

You rarely need a heavy hammer in the workshop for making small projects—a medium-weight hammer for general use along with a tackhammer (also called a warrington hammer) should meet all your needs. A mallet is also handy for striking chisels and persuading reluctant joints to cooperate.

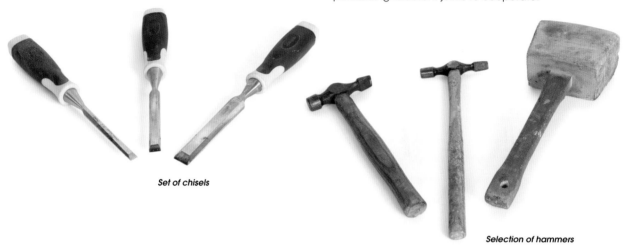

Set of chisels

Selection of hammers

SCREWDRIVERS

There are many designs of screwdriver and a variety of blades to fit different screw heads. A sensible choice is one with a ratchet handle and interchangeable bits so that you can deal with a range of types and sizes of screw.

CLAMPS

These are extraordinarily important—without them you will find it difficult to complete your projects. You need a good selection: bar clamps for panels and larger assemblies; speed clamps, 'F' clamps, and web clamps for all kinds of other jobs.

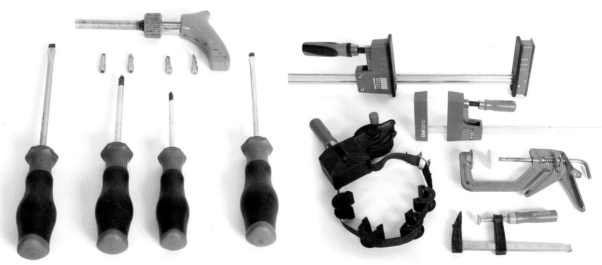

Selection of screwdrivers

Assorted clamps

POWER TOOLS

Power tools, whether corded or cordless and battery-powered, greatly speed up your woodworking. A power drill really is a necessity, and a jigsaw is another tool that is worth investing in, not only for its curve-cutting ability but also for its versatility with the wide range of blades that are available. A circular saw will make short work of cutting your boards. You can use it with a guide rail to improve accuracy.

POWER SANDER

A power sander eases the tedium of hand sanding and will give your projects a smooth, polished look. There are several different types of sander, but probably the most versatile is the random-orbit sander.

Random-orbit sander

SCREWDRIVER

For projects involving a lot of screw-driving, a powered screwdriver can be a real help. These are available in a variety of sizes to suit different jobs, but even the smallest are surprisingly powerful.

Cordless screwdrivers

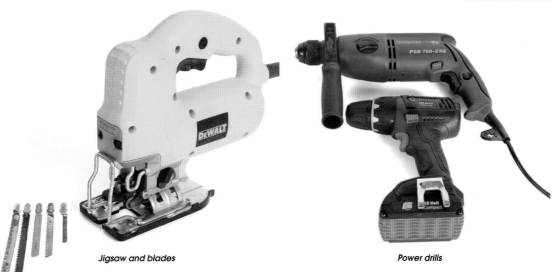

Jigsaw and blades

Power drills

ROUTER

For any serious woodworker, a router is the one tool that must be in the workshop. A router and router table allow you to undertake a wide variety of woodworking tasks, from shaping simple edge moldings to cutting joints. For these projects, a small router with a modest selection of bits will be enough; a simple router table will greatly simplify some operations.

Router

Biscuit jointer

BISCUIT JOINTER

The biscuit jointer is an extremely handy tool. It is simple and fast to use and can strengthen all manner of joints in moments. For all the projects in this book, No. 20 biscuits should be used unless otherwise noted.

WORKSHOP MACHINERY

If you become more serious about your woodworking, you will probably want to invest in some workshop machinery. This obviously demands a certain amount of workshop space and a fairly hefty financial outlay. However, it will raise your woodworking capabilities, allowing you to tackle large projects, and increase your speed and accuracy.

TABLESAW

The first machine that most woodworkers acquire is a tablesaw, perhaps the most important machine in the workshop. It can be used both to rip and crosscut boards and make angled and beveled cuts with ease and accuracy. The tablesaw is simply a circular saw mounted under a metal table. It is fitted with a pair of fences, one for ripping along the grain and a sliding fence for crosscutting. Some saws have a sliding table to support the wood more effectively when crosscutting. The crosscut fence may be rotated for cutting miters and other angled cuts, and the blade itself can be tilted for bevel cutting.

Tablesaw

BANDSAW

Along with the tablesaw, the bandsaw is also a good investment—in fact, many home woodworkers prefer bandsaws to tablesaws. This is attributable to several factors: first, bandsaws don't take up much floor space; second, they run quietly, unlike tablesaws, so they are less likely to annoy the neighbors; and finally, they are much less intimidating to use because there is no large spinning blade and consequently little danger of kickback (when a workpiece is caught by the blade and then hurled back at the operator). Bandsaws are particularly good for producing curved components and are great jointing machines. They are not as good as tablesaws at producing long straight cuts, but a well tuned bandsaw with a sharp blade will be able to do an acceptable job.

● ● ● ONE-BOARD TIP:

Cutting up the wood is just one of many jobs when making any project. You will also need to shape, joint, drill, and assemble the piece.

Bandsaw

COMBINATION SANDER

A combination sander is an enormously versatile tool. With a sanding belt and a sanding disc, it can be used for smoothing and shaping both curved and straight-edged components.

Combination sander

DRILL PRESS

A drill press greatly improves your drilling accuracy. Although a hand-held drill is fine for most jobs, when it comes to drilling perfectly accurate holes that are exactly perpendicular to the workpiece, you need some help. A drill press or a power drill mounted in a stand will do the job.

Power drill in a drill stand

CHAPTER TWO

TECHNIQUES

Woodworking is a disciplined process, and it is important to approach it methodically. If you work through projects logically, mistakes are less likely to occur. And as you familiarize yourself with various techniques, your skills will improve.

Start every project by selecting your materials and roughly marking out how to make the most economical use of them. Mark each board so that you know exactly where to cut each component. The next step is always to crosscut the components to length, then rip them to width. After that, you continue with planing, shaping, jointing, and assembling.

MEASURING AND MARKING

The first job on any project is to mark out your wood ready to be converted into the various components. It is easy to make mistakes at this stage that will affect the success of your project. There are few things more irritating than misreading a measurement and consequently cutting a board to the wrong size. The saying, "Measure twice, cut once," is certainly very good advice.

You need to be disciplined and methodical in your marking. First, check your measurements and make sure that you are using the correct system. Don't mix metric and customary, which can be easy to do by mistake, particularly if you have converted from one to the other.

Second, always use a clean, clear rule so that the markings are easy to see. Mark the board with a sharp pencil or marking knife, drawing it along a try square or a combination square. Carry the line around the wood to help you keep your saw cut straight. When you cut the wood, be sure you cut on the waste side of the line. This means that the marked line should still be visible on the cut component.

When making several identical pieces, do not measure each one separately, for this greatly increases the chances of making a mistake. Measure and cut the first piece, then use it as a template to cut the others. That way you can't go wrong, assuming that you managed to cut the first piece accurately. It is also a good idea to always start by cutting the longest components for a project. If you make a mistake it might still be possible to reuse the piece as one of the shorter components.

Professional woodworkers use devices called setting-out rods or story sticks, which are pieces of board onto which all the dimensions of a project are marked full scale. That way, the maker only needs to lay the story stick on the workpiece and mark off the correct dimensions—without any need for further measuring.

When marking curves and rounded edges, do not struggle with a compass. Instead, use a round object as a template—saucepan lids, paint cans, jars, and even coins are all good for this.

1 Mark across the face using a try square.

2 Carry the line around the edge.

3 Copy marks from one workpiece to another.

4 A pair of identically marked components.

SAWING

Most people know how to saw through a piece of wood, but it takes practice to do it accurately and consistently. The first thing is to use the correct grip. Don't hold the saw too tightly, and make sure that your index finger is pointing forward along the side of the blade. This helps to keep your forearm in line with the blade and make the sawing motion much more even.

To begin a cut, first place the blade on the wood on the waste side of the marked line. Use the thumb on your other, non-sawing, hand to support the blade. Pull the blade gently toward you. Repeat this once or twice until it has started to cut into the wood. Now move your thumb away and start to move the saw backward and forward in the cut, progressively increasing the length of the stroke until you are using the entire length of the blade. Keep an eye on the marked lines to ensure that you keep the cut accurate. Saw slowly and smoothly and let the saw do the work.

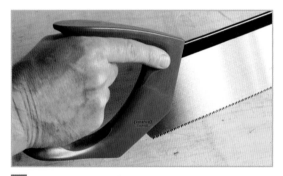

1 The correct saw grip.

2 Guide the saw with your thumb as you pull back to start the cut.

3 Once the cut is established, move your hand away and continue to saw through.

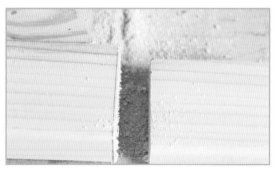

4 The completed cut. Note that the marked line is still visible on the workpiece.

WOOD CUTS

There are two different types of wood cuts. The first is rip cutting, which is when you cut parallel to the grain of the wood as you cut along a board. The second is crosscutting, which is when you cut across the grain of the wood as you cut a board to length. The two different cuts technically require two different saws. When you are ripping along the grain you are actually splitting the wood fibers apart, which needs large, coarse, widely spaced saw teeth. Crosscutting, however, severs the wood fibers and needs smaller, finer teeth to produce a good finish. These days, however, you can tackle both types of cut using a modern saw with hardened teeth; it has considerably more sophisticated tooth geometry than more traditional tools.

When cutting wood, you must keep it properly supported. For ripping large boards, sawhorses are traditionally used; alternatively, a portable workbench can do the job. For crosscutting smaller components on the bench, use a bench hook. This is a simple homemade jig with a cleat to support the wood as you cut it. For end-grain cutting, you can hold the wood in a bench vise.

A homemade bench hook

Ripping a board with the wood held in a portable workbench

SHARPENING YOUR TOOLS

Successful woodworking relies to a great extent on sharp, well-maintained tools. Blunt tools produce poor results and are far more likely to lead to accidents and mistakes. Their reluctance to cut easily makes you exert excessive pressure on them, causing them to slip, spoiling the work, and possibly injuring you. Tool sharpening is a subject that can, and does, fill entire books. However, for the purposes of this book, it is only necessary to cover the basic sharpening of planes and chisels.

When you buy a new plane or chisel, it will not be ready for immediate use without some initial preparation. The blade will leave the factory having only been fairly coarsely ground, but if you want it to produce a high-quality finish on the wood, it needs a razor-sharp edge. This is not difficult to achieve. All you need is a good, flat sharpening stone.

The initial grinding angle on the blade is normally 25 degrees. Some woodworkers simply polish this bevel and use the tool. But that means the blade has a rather weak edge, which can be easily damaged and will then be time-consuming to sharpen. I think that a better practice is to hone a secondary bevel on the blade at an angle of around 35 degrees. The advantage of this is that it produces a stronger edge and can be quickly resharpened, as only a tiny amount of metal will need to be removed.

1 A coarsely ground blade in need of honing.

2 To sharpen your blades, begin by flattening the back of the blade. Lubricate your stone, if necessary, then lay the blade on it, bevel up, and rub the blade along the stone while applying even pressure.

3 Continue until the back is smooth and evenly shiny.

4 Turn the blade over, bevel down, and rock the blade until you can feel that the bevel is flat on the surface. Now lift it slightly onto its tip in order to hone the secondary bevel. Keep the blade at this angle as you rub it up and down the stone.

5 Once you have managed to hone an even bevel about 1/32 in. (1mm) wide, stop. Now, if you feel the rear of the blade with your thumb, you will notice that you have raised a burr, which needs to be removed before the tool can be used. Do this by laying the blade down on the stone again, bevel up, and rub it a couple of times. Your blade is now ready for use. A really sharp blade should be able to shave the hairs from the back of your hand.

> **• • • ONE-BOARD TIP:**
>
> If you find it difficult to hold the blade accurately while you hone the secondary bevel, you can always use a honing guide. This is a small jig that attaches to the blade and holds it at the correct angle while you rub it along the sharpening stone.

PLANING

Once you have cut the wood, the next step is to plane it. This smooths the wood and removes any imperfections, such as the marks left by the saw blade.

SETTING UP YOUR PLANE

Planes are sophisticated tools and can appear a little intimidating to the novice. But, when properly sharpened and set up, a plane can be one of the most pleasurable tools to use as you sweep off wafer-thin shavings from the wood and expose a perfect surface.

1 The first thing to do when you get a new plane is to dismantle it, sharpen it, and set it up.

2 To reassemble a bench plane, first take the blade and hold it bevel down. Lay the cap iron across the blade so that the large screw drops through the hole in the blade.

3 Slide the cap iron up the slot and turn it so that it is correctly oriented on the blade.

4 Slide it down so that the front edge is about 1/32 in. (1mm) from the blade edge.

5 Tighten the screw using the lever cap. This assembly then sits on the frog, which is the sloping part on the top of the plane.

6 The cap iron is on top of the blade and then the lever cap is placed on top of the cap iron to hold everything in place. With the plane inverted, turn the blade-adjustment knob until the blade just protrudes through the sole. Use the adjusting lever to set the blade parallel to the sole. There should be a small gap in the sole just in front of the blade to allow the shavings to be ejected. The size of this gap can be adjusted by removing the blade assembly, loosening the frog, and moving it along the plane body.

USING A PLANE

Planing should not be hard work—the plane should slice cleanly through the wood without much resistance. You will need to adjust the blade to suit each board, but that just involves using the adjustment knob to set the blade protrusion.

1 Clamp the workpiece firmly in a vise or against a stop on the bench. Grasp the plane firmly by its handles and run it across the surface of the wood. Start with a little pressure on the front handle to initiate the cut and, as you move along the wood, transfer the pressure to the rear to avoid having the plane tipping downward as it finishes the cut. Try to plane the wood with the grain. You will achieve a much better finish with less risk of any rough spots.

2 To determine the correct planing direction, look at the side of the board. You should be able to see the angle at which the grain rises to the top. Plane in the same direction. Alternatively, if you run your finger along the top of the board in both directions, you should be able to feel that one feels a little smoother than the other. That is the direction to plane in.

CHISELING

In the home workshop, chisels can often be rather abused—they do, after all, look a bit like screwdrivers, and they are so good for opening cans of paint! However, that is not the way to treat your tools.

There are various kinds of chisels. The most common is the bevel-edged design, which has bevels on both its sides, making it versatile and useful in tight corners. Chisels are mainly used for chopping away waste material in joints, but they are also useful for shaping, trimming, cutting in hinges, and a variety of other jobs. The most important thing about a chisel is that it should be razor sharp. A sharp chisel will cut easily and produce a good finish with minimal effort, but a blunt chisel may tear the wood and needs considerably more force behind it to cut.

Contrary to popular belief, chisels are not always used with a mallet. Most often you will use just the power of your hand to propel the tool through the wood to pare away the waste. You would use a mallet when removing the waste from a mortise or cutting in a hinge. Whenever you use a chisel, make sure that the workpiece is properly secured in a vise or clamped to the workbench, and make sure that if the chisel slips it cannot injure you.

Always clamp your workpiece securely to the workbench and carefully pare away the waste.

POWER TOOLS

Although all the projects featured in this book can be made using hand tools alone, some power tools would make the job considerably easier. Here is a selection of the ones that can be most useful.

DRILL

The most familiar power tool is the drill, which can be bought very cheaply and is invaluable for drilling holes and running various useful accessories, such as sanding drums. Now, of course, battery-powered cordless versions are available, which are really convenient. You will also need a set of drill bits. Twist drills can be bought in both metric and customary sizes. It is important not to mix the two.

Power drills are relatively safe tools, provided you follow basic precautions. Make sure that the workpiece you are drilling into is securely clamped to the bench or held in a vise. Hold the tool tightly and make sure that you are drilling straight. If you are not sure, stand a try square on the bench to use as a guide. With corded drills, make sure that the power cord is safely out of the way so that you cannot trip over it or drill through it.

One particularly useful accessory is a drill stand. It helps ensure that your holes are perfectly accurate.

JIGSAW

The powered jigsaw takes the hard work out of cutting curved components. It can be used for both internal and external curves and can also cut a wide range of different materials when equipped with the right blade. Like any cutting tool, a jigsaw must be used with care. Always make sure that the power cord is above the workpiece so that there is no chance of cutting through it. Also check underneath the workpiece before you begin cutting. It is all too easy to clamp your work down and wonder why it is so hard to cut, only to find that you have been cutting into the bench as well.

The majority of modern jigsaws have variable-speed motors that are controlled by the trigger. This makes them easy to work even in inexperienced hands. The secret to using a jigsaw accurately is to make sure that you steer it carefully, pivoting around the blade. Never put any sideways pressure on the blade. That will produce a sloping, inaccurate cut that will spoil your work.

Cleaning up a curve with a drum sander mounted on a cordless drill

Cutting out a circular hole with a jigsaw

The finished hole

ROUTER

The router is an enormously capable machine that can perform a wide range of woodworking functions, including jointing, molding, shaping, and rabbeting. For the projects in this book, however, the router's use is mainly limited to some simple molding.

The router can appear intimidating to the novice with its exposed cutters and high-pitched whine, but once you understand its workings and the techniques for using it safely, you will find it is not a difficult machine to master.

There are two main components in the router: the body and the base. The body houses the motor, the variable-speed electronics, and the power switch. With a fixed-base router, you adjust the body to set the depth of cut, then lock the body in place. With a plunge router, the base supports the body on a pair of steel columns that allow the body to rise and fall as required to plunge the cutter into the workpiece.

Bits

Before using a router, you need to understand a little about the bits and how their rotation affects performance. The bit rotates in a clockwise direction when viewed from above, which means that if you plunge a bit into a workpiece and push the router away from you, it will have a tendency to pull to the left. So you must fit the side fence to the right-hand side of the tool to counteract this. However, some operators prefer to pull the router toward them; if that is your preferred method, you will need to fit the fence to the left-hand side of the router.

When using a router to profile an edge, where only one side of the bit contacts the workpiece, you must always work against the direction of rotation so that the router pushes back against you. This means if you were putting an edge profile around the outside of a workpiece, you would have to move the router in a counter-clockwise direction. But if, for example, you were profiling the inside of a frame, you would have to run the router clockwise.

Setting up your router

If you have not had much experience using a router, it is worth practicing some simple cutting on a piece of scrap wood or medium-density fiberboard (MDF) to get a feel for the machine.

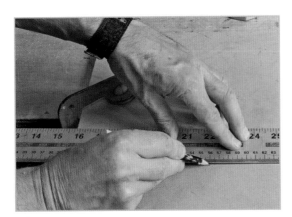

1 Clamp a short length of board to the workbench with its edge just overhanging the bench front. Draw a line parallel to the long edge about 4 in. (100mm) in from the front.

2 With the power disconnected, turn the router upside-down and fit it with a small straight bit about ¼ in. (6mm) in diameter. Make sure that at least three-quarters of the length of the cutter shank is inserted into the collet. Tighten securely.

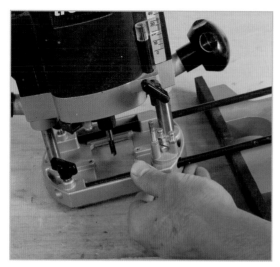

3 Now loosely fit the fence to the right-hand side.

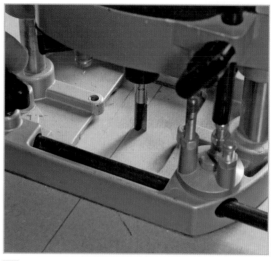

4 Stand the disconnected router on the workpiece and plunge the bit so that it just touches the surface. Engage the plunge lock and move the router until the bit is aligned with the marked line on the board. Adjust the fence so that it is tight against the front edge.

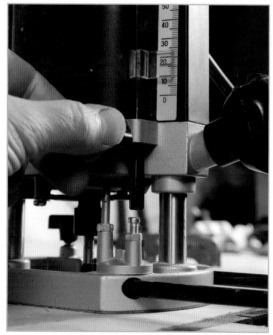

5 Now you must set the depth of cut. Leave the bit touching the workpiece and wind down the depth-adjusting rod until it touches the top of the turret on the base plate. Now zero the scale, if possible, and wind the rod up by 5/32 in. (4mm). Lock it in this position. Release the plunge lock on the router so that the body rises up on the posts, lifting the cutter off the surface.

6 Check the speed control. For a small-diameter bit like the one shown here, the router can be run at full speed. For larger-diameter bits, the speed should be reduced. Check that all the adjustment screws are tight on the fence and the depth-adjusting rod.

7 Position the router on the workpiece where you wish to start the cut. Make sure that the fence is hard against the edge. Grasp the router by both handles and start the motor. When it has reached full speed, press down on the handles to plunge the bit into the work. Engage the plunge lock and immediately start pushing the router forward to cut the groove.

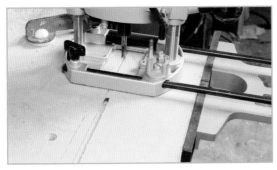

8 When you reach the end, release the plunge lock, allow the bit to rise out of the work, and switch off the motor.

> ● ● ● **ONE-BOARD TIP:**
>
> At first it can be difficult to tell how fast to move the router when making a cut. You should not force the machine along faster than it can cut, because that will strain the bit and the motor. The motor should run smoothly and the router should move forward easily. If you move too slowly, you will find that the bit overheats and leaves burn marks on the workpiece. When making particularly intricate cuts, it can be easier to move the router slowly. In that case, use the variable-speed control to reduce the bit speed.

Table routing

The router can also be used mounted beneath a router table. This method is particularly handy when shaping smaller components and when using large molding or jointing cutters that cannot safely be used in hand-held routing. The same set-up rules apply to table routing as to hand-held routing, although in this case the router remains stationary in the table and the workpiece is pushed past the bit, supported by a fence. It is important to use all the guards provided with the table, as they will protect you from the spinning cutter and also help support the work as it is machined.

A router table in action

BISCUIT JOINTER

The biscuit jointer is a very useful machine. It is fast and straightforward to use and very safe. It will cut strong joints in a moment, without the need for any complicated jigs or set-up. It is basically a small plunge saw that cuts a slot into which dried, compressed beech ovals, called biscuits, are glued. The application of a water-based glue such as PVA causes the biscuit to swell in the slot, creating a remarkably strong joint. Biscuits are ideal for edge-jointing when making up wide boards from narrow pieces. They can also be used instead of more complex joints, such as the mortise and tenon, in lighter construction.

Using a biscuit jointer is just a matter of adjusting the front fence so that the slot is cut in the center of the thickness of the wood. So if your board is ¾ in. (19mm) thick, set the fence to ⅜ in. (10mm). Be careful to hold the tool level when you cut the joint, otherwise the two halves will not line up properly.

When laying out biscuit joints, it is not critical that they be exactly spaced. You can just use a pencil and do it by eye—but be careful not to place biscuits too close to the ends of boards, as they can become exposed by subsequent trimming. Leave a gap of at least 2 in. (50mm).

1 Align the two boards to be joined and mark the biscuit positions.

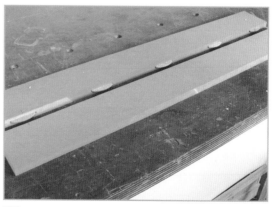

2 Mark the positions along the boards.

3 Clamp the boards to the edge of a bench and, holding the jointer horizontal, cut the joints.

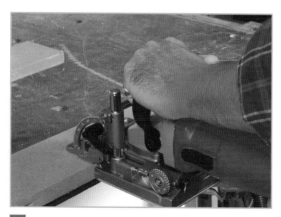

4 The boards ready for assembly.

5 To make corner joints, stand the two components together and mark the biscuit positions.

6 Cut the joints in the end of the side piece.

7 Then cut joints in the face of the end piece.

8 The joint is ready for assembly.

The completed joint

WORKSHOP MACHINERY

If you have the space, it's really worth investing in some workshop machinery. This will lift your woodwork to the next level and greatly improve your speed and accuracy.

TABLESAW

The tablesaw is the mainstay of the professional workshop, and any serious woodworker with a large enough workshop should have one. A good tablesaw will convert your boards into finished components in a short time and with little effort. It will save a considerable amount of time and trouble. However, a tablesaw is capable of inflicting serious injury on the unwary, so it must be used correctly.

Setting up a tablesaw

The saw must be set up according to the manufacturer's instructions. It should be standing on a level surface with space all around to give you room to work.

The guards must be properly set and should never be removed. There are two primary guards on newer table saws: the riving knife and the blade guard. (A riving knife is a rarity on older saws in the U.S.)

The riving knife is the curved metal piece that stands behind the saw blade. It holds the saw cut open after the board has passed the blade. The reason for this is that some wood can become case-hardened during the seasoning process, which means that when it is cut the internal stresses released can cause it to twist and move. If it should tighten around the back of the saw blade it can then be thrown back at the operator with considerable force. The riving knife protects you from this. It should be set about ⅛ in. (3mm) from the rear of the blade and should extend up to within ⅛ in. (3mm) of the top of the blade.

The blade guard is often mounted on the top of the riving knife and covers the upper part of the blade. It sometimes incorporates a dust-extraction outlet. Some blade guards are suspended over the blade without being attached to the riving knife.

Correctly set riving knife

Riving knife with an overhead guard fitted

Suspended blade guard

Using a tablesaw

The tablesaw performs two basic functions: ripping and crosscutting. Whenever you use a tablesaw you must use a fence—it is not safe to run a workpiece past the blade freehand. Never let your hands get anywhere near the spinning blade—it is always better to use a push stick.

Before using the saw, check your workpiece for any nails, screws, or loose knots. All these could damage the blade and will need to be removed. Next, set the fence. If ripping, the rip fence must be securely clamped and run exactly parallel to the blade. If crosscutting, the crosscut fence must be set at the correct angle. Start the motor and let the blade come up to speed, place the workpiece

Using too fine a blade or feeding the wood too slowly will result in burn marks.

against the fence and feed it smoothly past the blade. You should be able to feel how fast to feed the workpiece: too fast, and the motor will struggle and the quality of cut will be poor; too slow, and the blade will leave burn marks on the wood.

When ripping long boards, make sure that there is something to support the board as it comes off the back of the saw. Some saws have extension tables on the rear for additional support, while some people use a roller stand to support the wood. Alternatively, an assistant in the workshop could be the answer.

Check your fence accuracy with a try square.

BANDSAW

The bandsaw is another popular workshop machine, particularly in home workshops. There are several reasons for this. The bandsaw is a safer, quieter machine than the tablesaw. Because there is no heavy spinning blade and the main thrust of the blade is downward onto the table, there is no danger of kickback. The blade cuts a narrow kerf, meaning that there is less wood wasted, and it can also cut much thicker boards than a tablesaw.

Bandsaws can rip and crosscut and also cut curves. It is also safe to use them freehand without any fences. However, for all its good manners, it must be remembered that a bandsaw is still a dangerous machine capable of causing serious injury, so you must always keep your hands well away from the blade.

Setting up a bandsaw

Bandsaws are not difficult to set up once you understand the basics. The blade is a continuous steel band that runs over a pair of wheels. The first job is to ensure that the wheels track correctly and that the blade runs smoothly and stays true. Next, you need to adjust the blade tension. Then, finally, the guides must be set correctly to give the blade adequate support. This is how you do it.

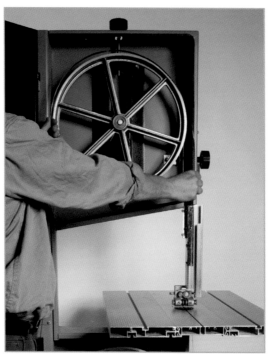

1 Unplug the saw and open the upper and lower doors. Loosen the blade guides above and below the table and slide them well away from the blade. Lower the upper blade guard so that it may be opened to release the blade. Release the tension on the upper wheel so that the blade is loose. Carefully lift the blade off the wheels and remove it. Wear gloves if you are worried about cutting your hands.

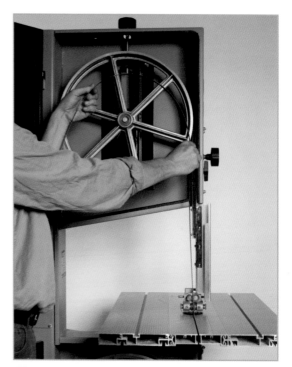

2 To fit a new blade, slide it into position and lift it onto the top and bottom wheels. Position it in the center of the tire and apply a small amount of tension until the wheels grip the blade.

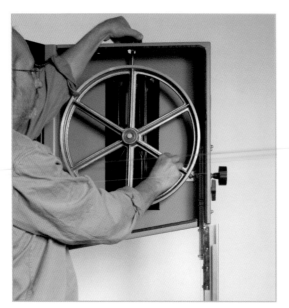

3 Now turn the top wheel clockwise by hand and watch the blade run on the top wheel. If it stays in the center, the tracking is correct; if it runs toward the front or the rear of the wheel then the tracking needs to be reset.

4 To reset the tracking, adjust the knob that is mounted on the rear of the upper casing. This tilts the upper bandwheel until the blade runs true. Once this is done, apply some more blade tension until the blade feels secure. The tension is about right when the blade deflects about ¼ in. (6mm) at the midpoint with the guides fully raised. Some larger bandsaws have an integrated blade-tension indicator, which simplifies the process.

5 The blade correctly centered on the bandwheel.

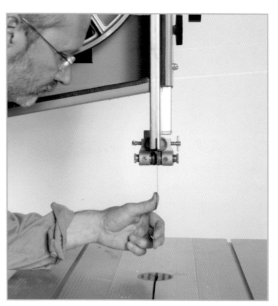

6 Checking the blade tension.

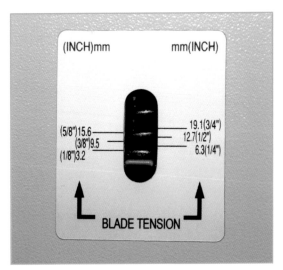

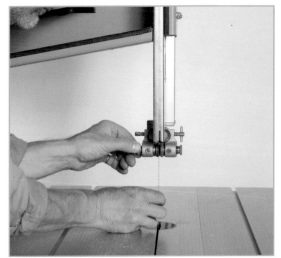

7 A blade-tension indicator is a great help.

8 Once you are sure that the blade is tracking correctly, move the guides into position. There are several different types of guide. Some manufacturers use plain metal guides, others use roller bearings. However, the same setting rules apply to both. The side guides should be set so that their front edges are just below the level of the blade gullets; they should be as close to the blade as possible without actually touching it.

9 The thrust bearing is the rear blade guide that supports the blade during cutting and stops it from being pushed off the bandwheels. Again, this should be set as close as possible to the back of the blade. It should only be in contact with the blade when the cut is taking place.

10 Once you are happy with the set-up, close the doors and start the machine. Let it run for a moment to check that all is well. While it is running, you can fine-tune the blade tension until the saw is running at its smoothest. It is worth checking that the motor drive belt is correctly tensioned. If your machine has several speeds, you should set it to the fastest speed for wood cutting. If the drive belt is too loose, it can slip and cause vibration; if it is too tight, it will put unnecessary strain on the belt itself and the wheel bearings.

11 Use a try square to check the accuracy of the fences.

12 Also check that the table is set at 90 degrees to the blade and adjust accordingly.

Using a bandsaw

Bandsaws are satisfying machines to use. With the wide variety of blades available, you can complete many tasks. Use wide blades when making long straight cuts and narrow blades for intricate curved work.

Set the upper saw guard so that the blade is covered as much as possible above the workpiece. This also brings the guide bearings down closer to the cutting point, increasing the accuracy of the cut. Start the machine and push the wood through at an even speed—do not force it, just let the machine cut at its own pace. Be careful when cutting curves not to twist the blade too much because you may damage it or pull it off the bandwheels. Also, when making deep cuts that involve withdrawing the blade from the workpiece after the cut is made, make sure you stop the machine before withdrawing the blade—otherwise, again, you may pull it off the bandwheels.

Occasionally you might find that a blade wanders, making it difficult to cut accurately. These problems are invariably caused by a worn or blunt blade, and replacing it with a new one should resolve it.

Curve cutting on the bandsaw

CHAPTER THREE

HEALTH AND SAFETY

The importance of workshop safety cannot be stressed too much. Careless use of sharp hand tools and electric power tools can lead to disaster. A poorly set up workshop can be a dangerous place, so take care to minimize the hazards with a little planning and some common sense.

WORKSHOP SAFETY

ELECTRICAL SAFETY

If you are using power tools or workshop machinery, you must make sure that both the tools and the electrical supply are safe. Your workshop wiring must conform to local regulations and have all the necessary protection systems installed. If you are in any doubt, you should have a licensed electrician check it over.

Power tools can also wear out over time and become faulty. The main thing that can cause problems is the power cord itself, which takes a lot of punishment. It can get pulled, stepped on, cut, and generally abused. Although cords are generally securely attached, they should be regularly checked and replaced when necessary. Never use a tool with a faulty cord. Keep your power tools and machines in good condition and always make sure that any safety guards are in place and working. Replace any worn parts and keep blades and bits sharp.

FIRST AID

It is worth keeping a small first-aid kit in the workshop with a few bandages and antiseptic cream, as even the most careful worker can sometimes cut a finger or get a splinter. Clean cuts do tend to bleed a bit—and you don't want bloodstains on your work.

PERSONAL PROTECTION

In the workshop it is important to wear and use certain protective gear to ensure your safety.

EAR PROTECTION

Woodworking can be noisy, particularly when using machines like a router or a planer. Protect your ears with a good set of hearing protectors or earplugs. Some people might not like the feeling of isolation that these create. To alleviate that problem you can use a set of hearing protectors with an integrated FM radio. These are a pleasure to wear.

A pair of standard hearing protectors

Hearing protectors with integrated FM radio

EYE PROTECTION

Even with all guards and protection in place, splinters and chips can still be thrown by power tools and other machinery. Powered jigsaws can be particularly problematic, because they cut from below the workpiece and eject the sawdust upward and straight into your eyes. A pair of safety glasses, or goggles if you prefer, will protect your eyes. You can buy some that will fit over prescription glasses—so there is no excuse not to wear them.

Reflective safety glasses   *Safety eyewear to go over prescription glasses*   *Pair of goggles*

PROTECTING YOURSELF FROM SAWDUST

One of the biggest problems in the workshop is sawdust. Not only does it make a mess but it is also extremely bad for your health if you inhale it, particularly if you use hardwoods.

Dust extraction

The solution to the problems caused by sawdust is to remove the dust at the source by dust extraction. This need not be complicated. Most dust-producing power tools are supplied with an adapter that can be connected to a shop vacuum. These are just industrial vacuum cleaners with special filters to capture the fine particles. They often also incorporate automatic switching systems, meaning that you connect your power tool to a socket mounted on the extractor, so that when you switch on the tool the extractor starts automatically.

For larger, stationary workshop machines, you will need a bigger dust collector with greater capacity. Many professional workshops have ducted extraction systems connected to all the machinery and controlled through a series of blast gates that direct the flow to the machine in use. This is an expensive option for the home woodworker, although it is more convenient than connecting the dust collector to each machine as you use it.

Workshop vacuum extractor

The power-tool socket and auto-switching controls on a shop vacuum

Large dust collector suitable for a ducted system connected to workshop machinery

Dust masks

Even with good dust extraction, there are times when you will still need to wear a dust mask. This is particularly important when working with MDF, which produces a very fine dust, and also some exotic hardwoods, which produce dust that can be highly irritating. There is a wide range of masks, from simple disposable ones through to sophisticated respirator masks fitted with motors that blow filtered air across your face. It is a matter of finding one that is right for you—for example, if you have a beard you may find that some masks don't seal well on your face. As a rule, for short periods, disposable masks are usually more than adequate.

Powered respirator with face shield

Disposable dust mask

Dust mask with replaceable filters

THE PROJECTS

BOOKENDS

Bookends are always useful. Here is a simple design with an art deco feel that can be made with either hand or power tools. This is also a good project for using up any offcuts you may have lying around the workshop, as the quadrants can be made from contrasting woods, which can look really attractive.

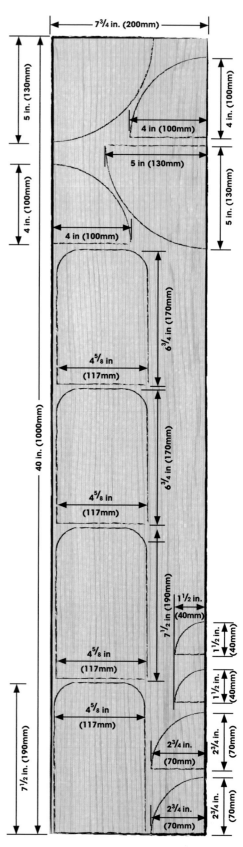

BOOKENDS

• • • YOU WILL NEED...

- Tablesaw or handsaw

- Jigsaw or coping saw

- Router table with straight bit

- Clamp

- Wood glue

Dimensions shown on the board diagram:

- 7³/₄ in. (200mm)
- 5 in. (130mm)
- 4 in. (100mm)
- 4 in. (100mm)
- 5 in. (130mm)
- 5 in (130mm)
- 4 in (100mm)
- 40 in. (1000mm)
- 6³/₄ in (170mm)
- 4⁵/₈ in (117mm)
- 6³/₄ in (170mm)
- 4⁵/₈ in (117mm)
- 7¹/₂ in (190mm)
- 4⁵/₈ in (117mm)
- 1¹/₂ in. (40mm)
- 1¹/₂ in. (40mm)
- 1¹/₂ in. (40mm)
- 4⁵/₈ in (117mm)
- 2³/₄ in. (70mm)
- 7¹/₂ in. (190mm)
- 2³/₄ in. (70mm)

Begin by marking out your board as shown here.

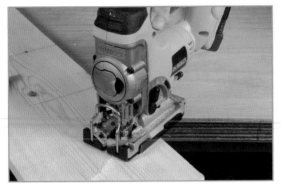

1 Prepare the board as described on page 19. The quadrants can be accurately cut with a powered jigsaw. Alternatively, you could use a fretsaw or coping saw.

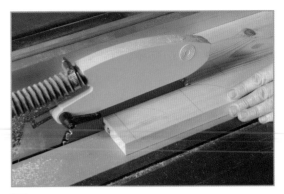

2 A tablesaw makes quick work of the other parts.

3 Take each pair of quadrants and clamp them together in a vise so that their square edges are aligned. Use a sanding block or a power sander to clean up the curved edge and smooth out any discrepancies.

4 The upright sits in a rabbet cut into the base. Stand the upright on the end of the base with the edges aligned. Mark the width of the board with a pencil.

5 Make the depth of the rabbet about two-thirds the thickness of the board.

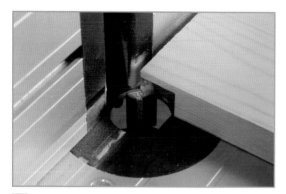

6 An easy way to cut the rabbet is to use a straight bit on a router table (as here). Alternatively, you can cut the rabbet using a tenon saw and chisel.

7 The corners of the bookends should be rounded. To do this, find something circular—a jar lid is ideal for the purpose—and position it on the corner. Mark the curve with a pencil.

8 There are various ways to round the corners. A disc sander is excellent. Alternatively, a bandsaw will do the job. If your bandsaw blade is too wide to make the curve, make some relief cuts around the curve first (as shown here), then the waste will fall away as you cut, freeing the rear of your blade. Clean up the curve with a sanding block.

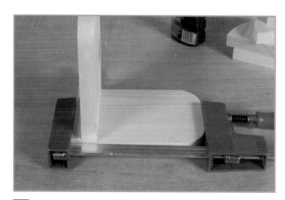

9 Apply glue to the rabbet and clamp the two components together. Make sure that they are set at right angles.

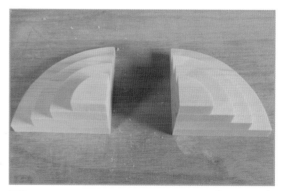

10 While the glue is curing, assemble the quadrants. These can be glued together in matching stacks. As long as the edges are square and the faces are smooth, apply a small amount of glue and simply stack the pieces. There is no real need to clamp them.

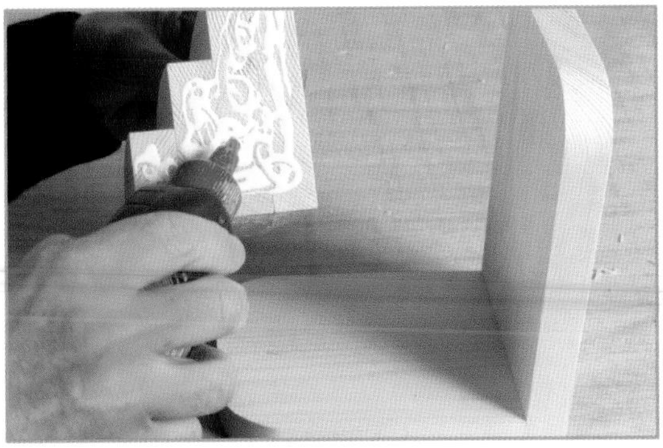

11 Finally, assemble the bookends, again with a little glue. The quadrants should be set back about 3/4 in. (19mm) from the front edge of the upright. Complete the project by softening all the edges with sandpaper, then apply your finish of choice.

• • • ONE-BOARD TIP:

When routing rabbets, remember to take several shallow passes, not one deep one.

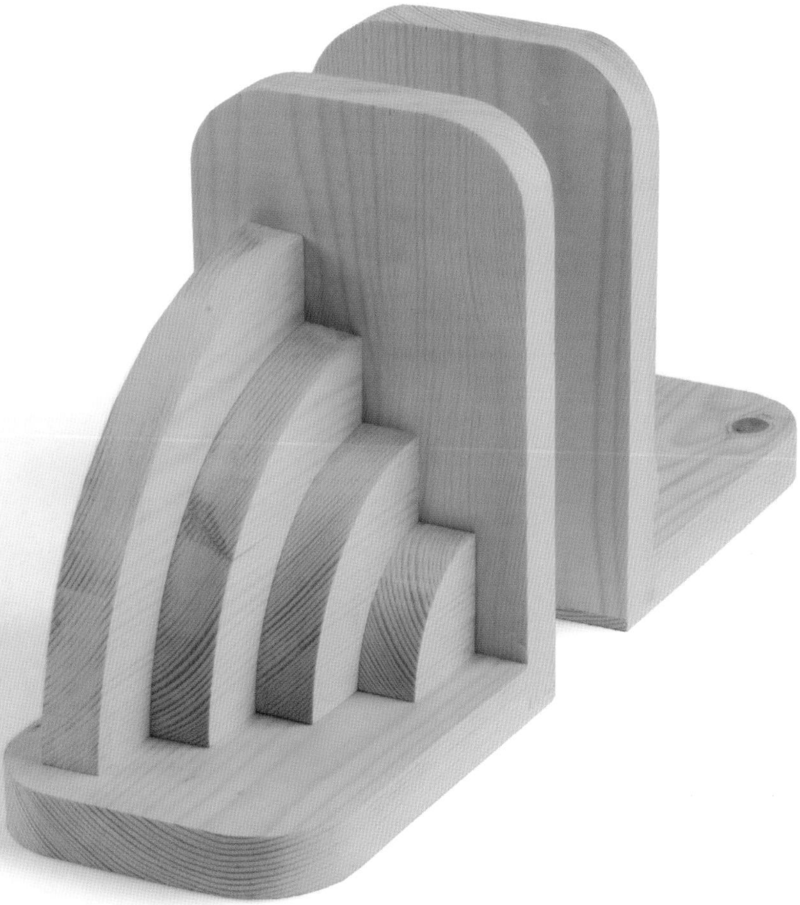

Your finished bookends should look like this when complete.

DISPLAY SHELVES

Here is a simple project to make a pair of display shelves. It involves a lot of curve cutting and some molding, for which you will need a router table.

The molding is purely for decoration, so leave it out if you prefer. However, do make sure that all the curves are smooth and that the corners are softened.

DISPLAY SHELVES

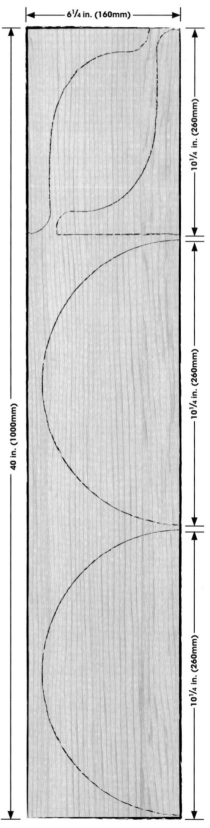

6¼ in. (160mm)

10¼ in. (260mm)

10¼ in. (260mm)

10¼ in. (260mm)

40 in. (1000mm)

Begin by marking out your board as shown here.
This plan shows components to make two display shelves.

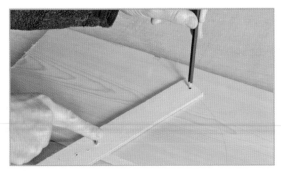

1 Prepare your board as described on page 19. To draw the large semicircles for the shelves, use a scrap of plywood with a hole for the pencil and a screw for a pivot. Draw both shelves, but only draw the bracket for one. To do this, try to produce a pleasing freehand curve. This might take a few attempts.

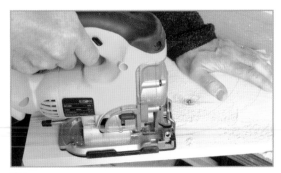

2 Cut out the shelves using a jigsaw or bandsaw. Alternatively, you could use a coping saw.

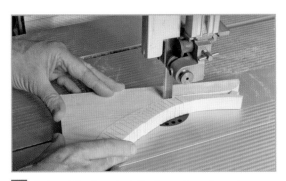

3 Cut out the bracket. If using a bandsaw, be sure to make some relief cuts so that the waste falls away as the cut progresses. Otherwise, the blade can get twisted, particularly if it is on the wide side.

4 Smooth the inside curve of the bracket. A drum sander is ideal for this job.

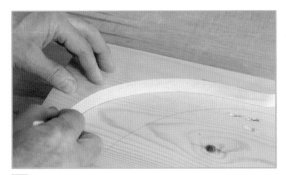

5 Once you have sanded the bracket into a nice smooth curve, use it as a template to mark out the second bracket.

6 There are several ways to match up and create identical components. Here, both shelves are clamped in the vise so they can be sanded or planed together to smooth out the curves and remove the saw marks.

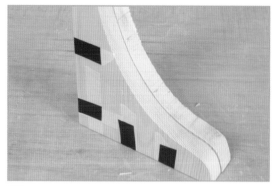

7 Another option is to use one piece as the template for the other. Here, the finished bracket and the sawn bracket are taped tightly together.

8 A bearing-guided straight-cut router bit is then used on the taped brackets, with the bearing riding on the finished bracket and the cutter shaping the sawn bracket to match.

9 Mold the edge of the shelf, again using a bearing-guided bit. An ogee cutter was used in this example.

10 The finished profile.

11 This is a corner-bead bit, which is a useful decorative tool. Use it to run a bead down each side of the bracket.

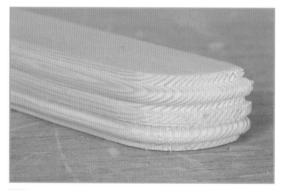

12 Do one pass on one side and one on the other.

13 Now the shelf can be assembled. Measure and mark the center line across the underside of the shelf.

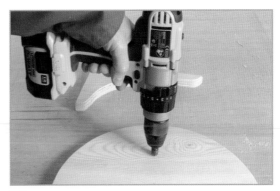

14 Drill two 5/32-in. (4-mm) holes through from the underside, on the line. Turn the shelf over and countersink the holes.

15 Put the bracket in the vise. Line it up carefully with the marked line, with its back flush with the back edge of the shelf. Attach it with a pair of screws.

16 For neatness, you can fill the screw holes with wood filler. Sand the filler flush when dry.

17 To hang the shelves, use a pair of wall hangers on each one. Chisel out a small recess in the shelf back so that the hanger does not hold it away from the wall. Screw the hangers in place.

Your finished display shelf should look like this when complete.

TOY ROCKING CHAIR

Here is a design for a small rocking chair, ideal for the average teddy. However, there is no reason why you could not scale up the components to make a larger chair to suit a child. Drawing out the curved sides can be a bit of a challenge. An easy method is to take a sheet of paper and draw some experimental curves. When you find a shape you like, you can transfer it onto the wood by scribbling on the back face of the paper under the curve. Then lay the paper on the wood and draw along the curve again, transferring the outline onto the board.

TOY ROCKING CHAIR

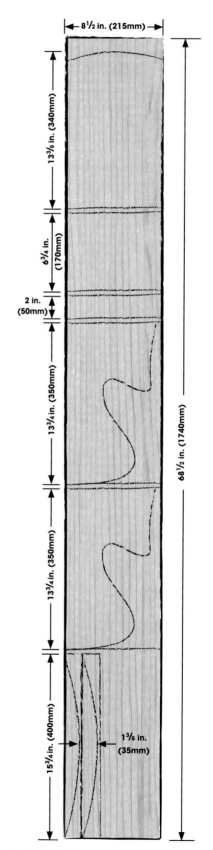

8½ in. (215mm)

13⅜ in. (340mm)

6¾ in. (170mm)

2 in. (50mm)

13¾ in. (350mm)

13¾ in. (350mm)

68½ in. (1740mm)

15¾ in. (400mm)

1⅜ in. (35mm)

Begin by marking out your board as shown here.

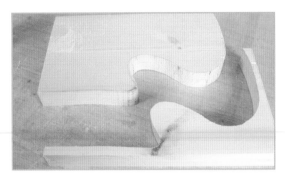

1 Prepare your board as described on page 19. Once you've cut the wood, clamp both sides together and cut out the curve using a jigsaw (as shown here) or a coping saw.

2 The completed cut.

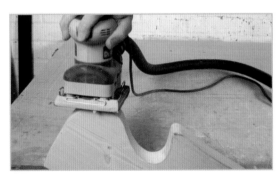

3 However good your cutting, the edges will still need smoothing. Use a drum sander on the inside curve.

4 And use a random-orbit sander on the outside curve.

5 The chair needs to sit at an angle on the rockers. Mark a point 1 in. (25mm) up from the rear corner of the side piece. Draw a line from the front corner up to that point.

6 You can cut both pieces at the same time by stacking them on the tablesaw (as here) and using an angled crosscut fence. Alternatively, you can cut them separately using a handsaw.

7 The curve for the rockers has a radius of 24½ in. (620mm). To mark this, you can put a nail in your bench and use a long ruler or a piece of string to draw the curve.

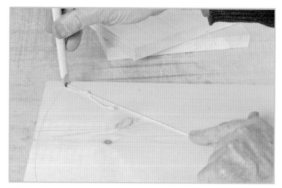

8 Cut the back panel roughly to length and mark a curve across its top. To do this, make a mark on each side 1 in. (25mm) from the top. Then, using a piece of string pivoting around the center of the board, draw a curve through these two points and as close to the top edge as possible.

9 Cut out the rockers using a jigsaw or bandsaw (as here).

10 Clamp both rockers together and smooth them evenly on a belt sander.

11 Round the ends of the rockers on a disc sander.

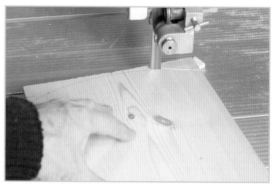

12 Use the bandsaw again to cut the curve on the top of the rear panel.

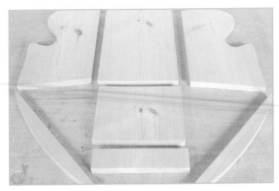

13 All the components, including the seat and apron, are now cut out and ready for assembly.

14 Before assembling the chair, round over the edges of the main components. Use a bearing-guided roundover bit mounted in a router table.

15 Carefully run the bit around the front edges of the side panels, the top of the rear panel, the front edge of the seat, and the bottom edge of the apron.

16 The back and sides are assembled using biscuit joints. Mark the positions.

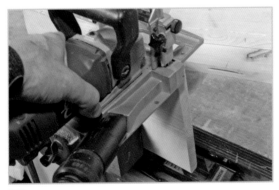

17 Cut the slots with a biscuit jointer.

18 Apply a little glue to the slots and insert the biscuits. Apply a little glue to the slots on the adjoining piece.

19 Assemble the back and sides and clamp up. Leave to dry.

20 The apron is attached to the underside of the seat, again using biscuits. Set it back about ¼ in. (6mm) from the front edge. Glue and clamp up.

21 The seat is held in position with pocket screws. Use a jig to drill two holes in each side.

22 Slide the seat into position and drive in the screws.

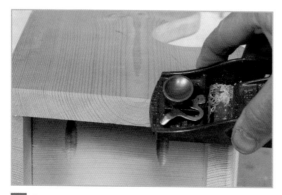

23 The rockers will be joined to the sides using biscuit joints. To disguise any discrepancies in the joint and to provide a straight shadow line, use a block plane to form a small chamfer on the bottom edge. You can also do the same on the outer edge of the rocker.

24 Mark the position of the biscuits on the sides and the rockers, then cut the slots.

25 Apply glue to the joints, assemble, and clamp up.

26 You now have the completed chair. Carefully hand sand it to remove any rough edges and blemishes.

Your finished rocking chair should look like this when complete.

KNIFE BLOCK

Kitchen knives can be difficult to keep handy yet store safely. One of the most convenient ways to do so is to use a knife block like the ones supplied with expensive sets of knives. This is a surprisingly easy thing to make, which you can adapt to suit your own collection of knives.

KNIFE
BLOCK

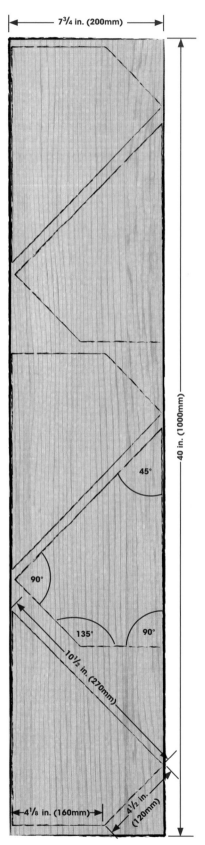

Begin by marking out your board as shown here.

1 Prepare your board as described on page 19. Cut out the parts with a tablesaw or handsaw. There will inevitably be slight discrepancies between the parts, so clamp them all together in a vise and clean them up with a smoothing plane.

2 Use a block plane on the end grain.

3 Stand all the pieces together and mark a 'V' across the front so that you can reassemble the pieces in the right order after routing.

4 Mark out in pencil the positions of the knives you want to house in the block. Allow enough space so the blades will slide in and out easily. Start with the outer piece.

5 Then put the next piece on top and repeat the exercise.

6 Continue this process until the block is complete.

7 Extend the marked lines with a ruler and clearly indicate the areas to be cut out. These odd-shaped parts are difficult to rout using any kind of clamp, so position one of the parts on the front of the bench so that its edge just overlaps. Take a pair of wood or MDF offcuts and temporarily nail them onto the bench top to hold the piece in place.

8 Fit the router with the straight bit. Set the cutting depth by plunging the cutter onto a flat surface, and then loosely sandwich one of the knife blades between the depth stop and the turret. Lock the depth stop.

9 Attach the router's guide fence and use the front edge of each of the pieces to guide the tool as you rout out all the knife slots.

10 Apply glue to the pieces, being careful to avoid the knife slots.

11 Use the 'V' marking to ensure that you are reassembling the block in the right order, then clamp tightly. Allow the glue to set overnight.

12 When dry, clean up the combined piece with a random-orbit sander.

ONE-BOARD TIP:

To keep the block clean, it is a good idea to give it a couple of coats of varnish or oil. As a final touch, fit the base with a set of adhesive rubber feet to protect your work surface.

13 Finish by rounding over all the edges, using the router fitted with a bearing-guided roundover bit. A non-skid mat on the bench should hold the block securely. Alternatively, you could round the edges with a power sander.

Your finished knife block should look like this when complete.

UMBRELLA STAND

In the past, no hallway would have been complete without an umbrella stand. Often an exotic and decorative object, it would be used to hold walking sticks and other paraphernalia as well as umbrellas. Here is a simple design to make a hexagonal stand. In order to cut the angles for the joints accurately, ideally you would need a good tablesaw. However, if you do not have one, you can cut the joints by hand and use a plane to smooth the edges to the correct angle.

UMBRELLA
STAND

• • • YOU WILL NEED...

- Tablesaw or handsaw

- Biscuit jointer and biscuits

- Block plane

- Band clamps

- Router

- Bandsaw, jigsaw, or coping saw

- Drill

- Screwdriver

- Wood glue

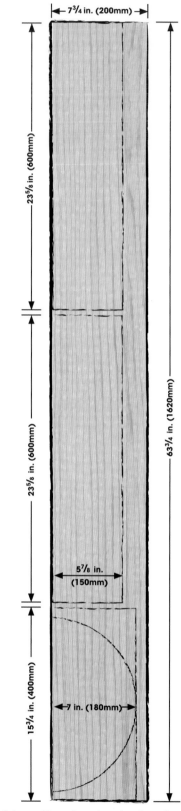

7³/₄ in. (200mm)

23⁵/₈ in. (600mm)

23⁵/₈ in. (600mm)

5⁷/₈ in. (150mm)

15³/₄ in. (400mm)

7 in. (180mm)

63³/₄ in. (1620mm)

Begin by marking out your board as shown here three times.
Note that your board must be long enough for
six rectangular shapes and two semicircles.

1 Prepare your board as described on page 19. Once you have marked up and crosscut the board, you need to rip the edges of each side to an angle of 60 degrees. This must be accurately set, as any tiny discrepancy becomes magnified over six joints. The simplest way is to use a protractor and a sliding bevel to set your saw blade. However, if you have mislaid your protractor, there is another method. First, take a board offcut and draw a line parallel to one straight edge.

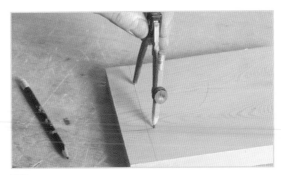

2 Then, take a compass and set the width about three-quarters of the length of the marked line. Mark an arc on the line and another above.

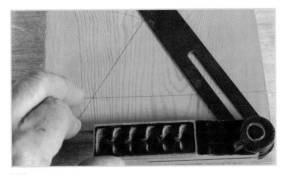

3 Using the same setting, place the compass point where the arc and the line intersect and draw an arc on the other end of the line and another to intersect the upper arc.

4 Use a ruler to join the three points and you will have an equilateral triangle, the internal angles of which are all 60 degrees.

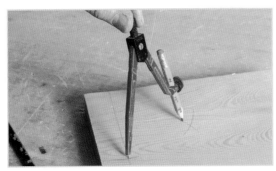

5 Use the triangle to set the sliding bevel.

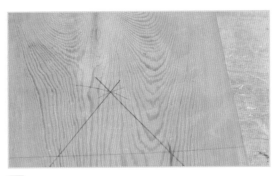

6 Use the bevel to tilt the saw blade to the correct angle.

7 Rip the first side of the board, with the fence set slightly wider than the finished width. You do this because you are going to cut the other side, and will need a little extra width to allow the saw to cut the bevel there.

8 Now set the fence to the exact width, turn the board around, and rip the other edge. Repeat these two steps for all six sides.

9 Lay all the side panels edge to edge on the bench, with their outer faces down and their ends lined up. Mark two horizontal lines, one 3 in. (75mm) from the bottom and one 3 in. (75mm) from the top. These will be used to locate the biscuit joints.

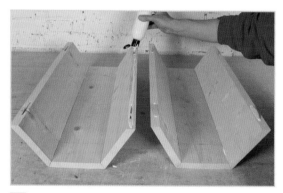

10 With the panels still lying face down on the bench, cut a biscuit slot at each end on the pencil line.

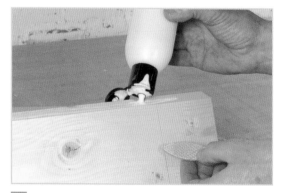

11 Apply glue to the edges and into the biscuit slots, making sure that there is sufficient glue in the slots. Insert the biscuits and begin the assembly.

12 Assemble two sets of three panels.

13 Fit the two sets of panels together.

14 Clamp together. Clamping up this kind of assembly is tricky, and the easiest method is to use web clamps or roof-rack straps. Wrap them tightly around the panels. Make sure the joints are tight and the shape is true. Leave until the glue has cured.

15 After removing the straps, you will find that the corners are all very sharp. Use a block plane to smooth them down a little.

16 To form a chamfer around the edge of the stand, fit a bearing-guided chamfer bit in the router (as shown). If you do not have a router, use a block plane instead.

17 Lay the stand on its side and carefully run the router around the top edge to cut the chamfer.

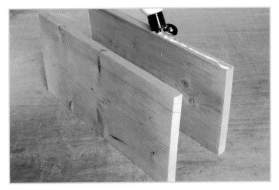

18 The base of the stand is made from a pair of boards joined together. You can use biscuit joints if you like, but they are not really necessary. Just make sure that the two joining edges fit neatly without any gaps.

19 Use a pair of bar clamps to hold the boards while the glue cures.

20 Mark out the shape of the base on the board. The example here is a 14-in. (360-mm) -diameter circular base—marked out with a compass—but a hexagonal base to match the stand will also work well.

21 A bandsaw was used to cut out this circle, but a jigsaw or coping saw could also be used.

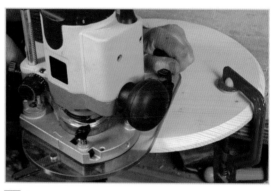

22 To match the chamfer on the top of the stand, use the same cutter to run around the base. If you have an extended router base, it will make the router more stable and easier to control.

23 Stand the main body on the base and center it by measuring in from the edge of the base to the corners of the stand.

24 Mark its position inside and out.

25 Remove the stand from the base and drill a clearance hole in the top of the base in the center of where each panel will be positioned.

26 Countersink the holes on the bottom of the base. Invert the stand and place the base on top of it. Carefully line it up with the marks and then drive the six screws.

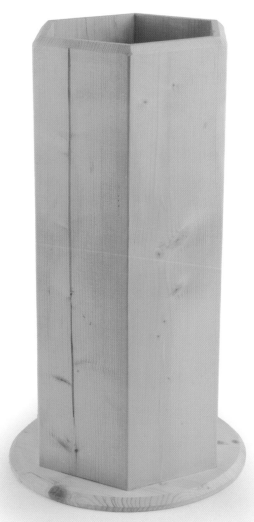

Your finished umbrella stand should look like this when complete.

KITCHEN SHELVES

You need a lot of storage space in a kitchen, and there are often little corners where you can fit a set of shelves. Here is a simple design that incorporates a rail for towels. It could be used for crockery or perhaps as a spice rack. The shelves have high front edges to prevent things from slipping off. A chrome hanging rail was used here, but a length of dowel will do equally well.

KITCHEN SHELVES

- Tablesaw or handsaw

- Router and straight-cutting bit

- Router table

- Chisel

- Jigsaw or coping saw

- Disc sander

- Clamps

- Length of chrome hanging rail or
  hardwood dowel

- Wall hangers

- Wood glue

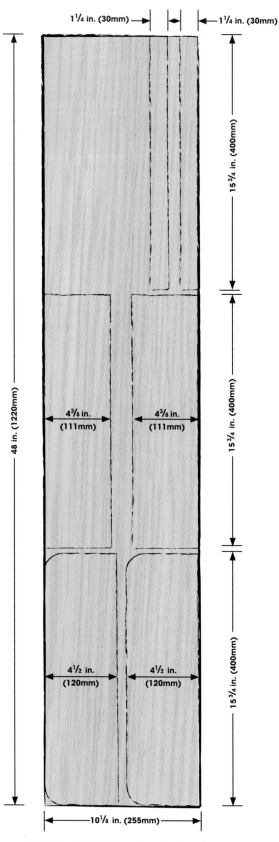

1¼ in. (30mm)   1¼ in. (30mm)

15¾ in. (400mm)

4⅜ in. (111mm)   4⅜ in. (111mm)

15¾ in. (400mm)

4½ in. (120mm)   4½ in. (120mm)

15¾ in. (400mm)

48 in. (1220mm)

10⅛ in. (255mm)

Begin by marking out your board as shown here.

1 Prepare your board as described on page 19. Mark out the components. Both the sides and the shelves are the same length.

2 The shelves are narrower than the sides, so rip ⅛ in. (3mm) off the width. Also cut the two shelf fronts, but leave them overlong at this stage so you can trim them to fit accurately later.

3 Lay one shelf on top of one side panel and, with the rear edges lined up, mark the width of the shelf on the side. Repeat with the other side panel.

4 Mark the shelf positions on the side panels with a single line. They are set at 4 in. (100mm) from the ends of the sides. A good tip is to scribble on the side of the line where the dado is to be cut to avoid making a mistake and cutting on the wrong side. Lay both side panels on the bench, back to back, so that the shelf-width marks that you made are on the outside edges and the shelf positions are lined up. Lay a board across the bottom.

5 The board will guide the router when cutting the dadoes. Insert a ½-in. (12.5-mm) -diameter straight-cutting bit in the router and set the depth of cut to ¼ in. (6mm). Clamp the board tightly across the end panels so the router runs exactly along the edge of the marked line. Cut the joint, being careful not to run over the end lines. Work from right to left. Then repeat the process for the second shelf.

6 The ends of the dadoes need to be squared off to match the shelves. Use a chisel for this.

7 The ends of the side panels are rounded. Use any convenient circular object as a template.

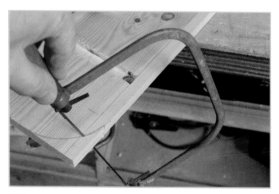

8 Cut off the corners using a coping saw (as here) or a jigsaw.

9 Smooth the curves on a disc sander.

10 The towel rail sits in a pair of holes bored into—but not through—the side panels. Mark the position of these 2 in. (50mm) in from the back and 2 in. (50mm) from the bottom.

11 Because the sides are thin, a flat bit cannot be used to bore the hole, so use the router instead. Fit a cutter to match your rail—a ¾-in. (19-mm) straight-cutting bit was used here. Set the depth of cut to ¼ in. (6mm). Set the router fence to 2 in. (50mm) from the center of the bit. Position the router on the side panel and then use a clamp to hold it in place while you bore the hole.

12 The front edges of the side panels and the tops of the shelf fronts need to be rounded over. Fit a bearing-guided roundover bit in your router table.

13 Set the fence flush with the bearing.

14 Carefully round over the front, top, and bottom edges of the side panels on both sides.

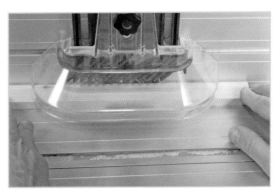

15 Round over the top edges of the shelf fronts.

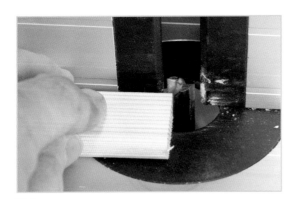

16 It is worth cutting a rabbet on the back of the shelf fronts. This makes assembly easier and provides a neater finish. Fit a straight bit in the router table and set the height to the thickness of the board.

17 Align the fence so that the bit will cut a rabbet that is ¼ in. (6mm) deep.

18 This is a tricky cut to make because the workpiece is rather narrow, so use featherboards to hold it securely against the bit.

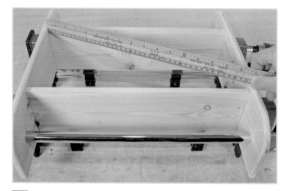

19 Assemble the unit without glue to make sure that it all fits together. The towel rail should be the same length as the shelves. Hold it all together with clamps. Check the diagonals to ensure that the unit is square.

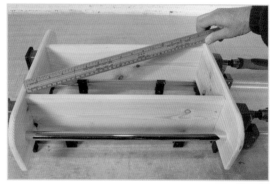

20 The diagonals should be equal. If they are not, loosen the clamps and adjust them to pull the frame into shape.

21 Position the shelf fronts and mark the correct length. Cut them to size.

22 Dismantle the frame and apply glue to the joints, then glue on the shelf fronts.

23 Reassemble, clamp up, and allow the glue to dry.

ONE-BOARD TIP:

Always check projects for squareness when gluing and clamping, as it is all too easy to over-tighten the clamps and push the assembly out of shape.

24 To attach the unit to the wall, screw a pair of hangers to the rear of the top shelf.

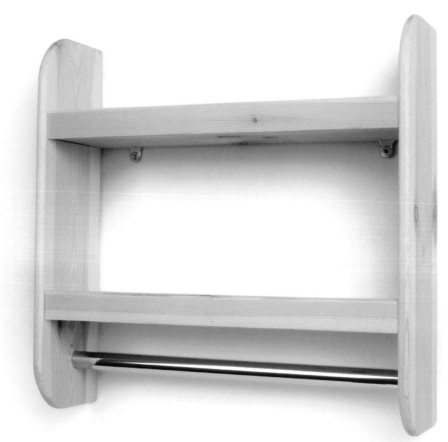

Your finished kitchen shelves should look like this when complete.

BATH RACK

There are few things nicer than a long soak in a hot bath after a hard day's work. To help you make the most of your bath-time experience, here is a simple design for a bath rack that can hold all the necessities and perhaps prop up a book as well. It is a fairly simple project to make, although there are some repetitive tasks where simple jigs or guides can help.

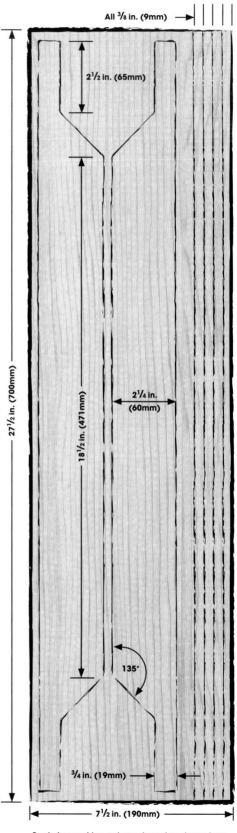

All ³⁄₈ in. (9mm)

2¹⁄₂ in. (65mm)

2¹⁄₄ in. (60mm)

18¹⁄₂ in. (471mm)

27¹⁄₂ in. (700mm)

135°

³⁄₄ in. (19mm)

7¹⁄₂ in. (190mm)

Begin by marking out your board as shown here.

BATH RACK

● ● ● YOU WILL NEED...

- Tablesaw or bandsaw

- Router table with roundover bit

- Sander

- Drill

- Screwdriver

1 Before you begin, check the measurements against the width of your bathtub and make any necessary adjustments. Prepare your board as described on page 19. Start by cutting out the two side pieces. A bandsaw is ideal for this (as here), although a jigsaw or a handsaw would be fine.

2 Use a miter fence to make the angled cuts.

3 Mount a bearing-guided roundover bit in your router table.

4 Machine the top edges of both sides.

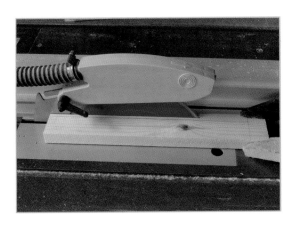

5 The next job is to make the slats. These should be ³⁄₈ in. (9mm) thick and 6¹⁄₄ in. (160mm) long. Rip several lengths off the board. To be safe, you should always use push sticks when ripping narrow sections.

6 Crosscut the slats to length. You will need 20.

7 The slats will be attached to the sides with screws. This means that they must all be drilled and countersunk at both ends. If you have a drill press, clamp a couple of offcuts to the table to act as guides to hold the slats in position. For best results, use a $^5/_{32}$-in. (4-mm) drill bit with a countersink.

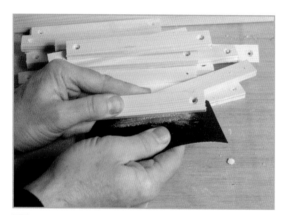

8 Now all the slats must be carefully sanded. Unfortunately, the only way to do this is by hand. Take care to remove all sharp edges and corners.

● ● ● **ONE-BOARD TIP:**

When making several identical components, do not measure each one separately, but instead cut one accurately and use it as a template to mark out the rest.

To prevent bath water from spoiling the wood, seal it with clear varnish or finishing oil.

9 The slats are attached with no. 6 x ¾-in. (no. 6 x 19-mm) screws. Start attaching the ones on each end, which will then hold the sides in position. Then simply arrange the remaining slats evenly along the rack. You can do this purely by eye, although if you want the spacing to be perfect you will have to work out the gap and make a spacer piece.

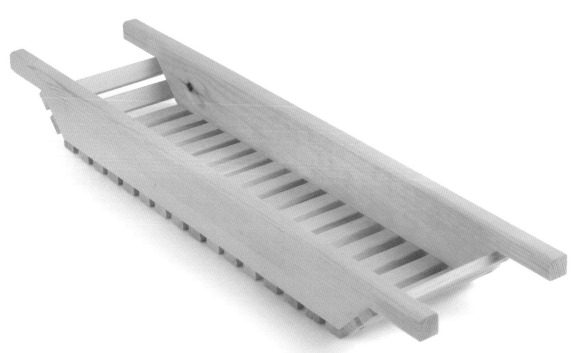

Your finished bath rack should look like this when complete.

LAMP BASE

Table lamps can be remarkably expensive, so why not make your own?

Of course, many people choose to turn their lamp bases, but if turning is not

your forte you need an alternative plan. Here is a simple design that is pretty easy to

make. You will need to buy the electrical components and some paint. A length

of $^5/_{16}$ in. (8mm) threaded rod will also be helpful. Apart from that, you just need a

board. Choose a nice piece of hardwood if you can. The plan here shows

components to make a pair of lamps.

LAMP BASE

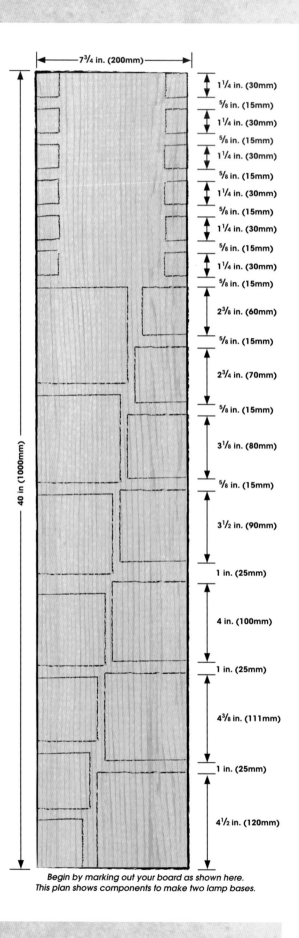

7³/₄ in. (200mm)

40 in (1000mm)

1¹/₄ in. (30mm)
⁵/₈ in. (15mm)
1¹/₄ in. (30mm)
⁵/₈ in. (15mm)
1¹/₄ in. (30mm)
⁵/₈ in. (15mm)
1¹/₄ in. (30mm)
⁵/₈ in. (15mm)
1¹/₄ in. (30mm)
⁵/₈ in. (15mm)
1¹/₄ in. (30mm)
⁵/₈ in. (15mm)
2³/₈ in. (60mm)
⁵/₈ in. (15mm)
2³/₄ in. (70mm)
⁵/₈ in. (15mm)
3¹/₈ in. (80mm)
⁵/₈ in. (15mm)
3¹/₂ in. (90mm)
1 in. (25mm)
4 in. (100mm)
1 in. (25mm)
4³/₈ in. (111mm)
1 in. (25mm)
4¹/₂ in. (120mm)

Begin by marking out your board as shown here.
This plan shows components to make two lamp bases.

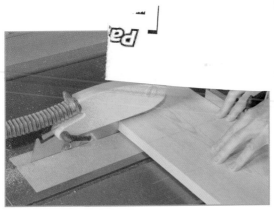

1 Prepare your board as described on page 19. Any type of saw can be used to cut out the parts. Here, a tablesaw is being employed.

2 A bandsaw is particularly good for cutting out the smallest squares.

3 Clean up all the edges with sandpaper. Round the corners and soften all the edges so the parts are smooth to the touch.

4 Each block needs a $5/16$-in. (8-mm) hole drilled through its center. Here a hand drill is used. It is important that this hole be accurately positioned and bored at precisely 90 degrees.

5 For greater accuracy, use a drill press or a power drill in a stand, if you have one.

6 To facilitate this, you can make a simple jig, as here, to hold all the small blocks in position for drilling.

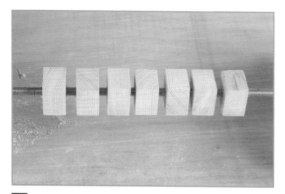

7 All the small blocks need to be painted black, so slide them onto the threaded rod.

8 Support the rod on blocks or small boxes and paint the edges.

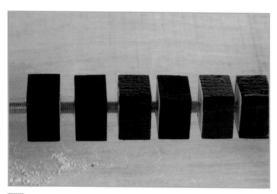

9 Leave to dry.

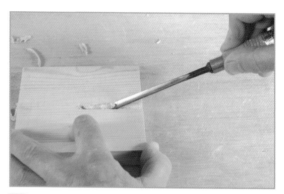

10 To accommodate the electrical cord, you need to cut a groove in the underside of the base. A small carving gouge was used here, but a router fitted with a core-box bit would also do a good job.

11 The finished groove. Check that it is deep enough to contain the cord.

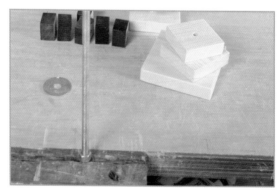

12 To assemble the lamp, clamp the threaded rod in the vise with a nut and large washer at the bottom.

13 Slide the base onto the rod so that it seats on the washer. Put a small amount of glue around the center and then slide a black block down onto it.

14 Continue this process until the pieces are all on.

15 Experiment with different alignments if you like.

16 Once you are happy with the set-up, put another large washer on the top and screw a nut down tight on the assembly to hold it together while the glue cures.

17 Once the glue has cured, the rod can be removed. It can be a little reluctant to come out and may need a few taps with a hammer. Be careful to support the assembly properly so it is not damaged. Insert the cord and fit the lamp holder.

Your finished table lamp should look like this when complete.

LAPTOP TRAY

Laptops are amazing machines, allowing you to work or play wherever you are. However, actually using them on your lap for any length of time can become uncomfortable—the base can get hot, and it can be cramped staring down at the screen—and some health issues have been associated with doing so. Here is a design for an adjustable tray that will allow you to use your laptop anywhere in comfort.

LAPTOP TRAY

● ● ● YOU WILL NEED...

- Tablesaw or handsaw

- Plane

- Biscuit jointer

- Biscuits

- Hand sander

- Disc sander

- Drill

- Hammer

- Wood glue

- Four $^{5}/_{16}$-in. (8-mm) T-nuts

- Four $^{5}/_{16}$-in. (8-mm) wing nuts

- Four $^{5}/_{16}$- x 2-in. (8- x 50-mm) bolts and washers

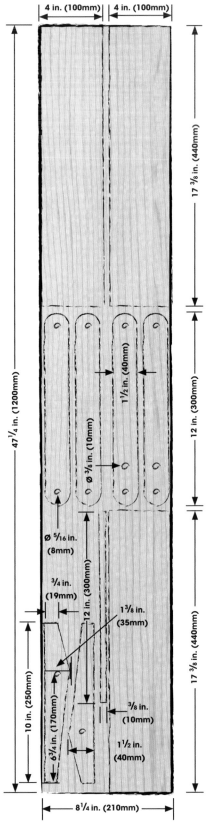

4 in. (100mm)   4 in. (100mm)

17 $^{3}/_{8}$ in. (440mm)

47 $^{1}/_{4}$ in. (1200mm)

12 in. (300mm)

1 $^{1}/_{2}$ in. (40mm)

Ø $^{3}/_{8}$ in. (10mm)

Ø $^{5}/_{16}$ in. (8mm)

$^{3}/_{4}$ in. (19mm)

12 in. (300mm)

1 $^{3}/_{8}$ in. (35mm)

17 $^{3}/_{8}$ in. (440mm)

$^{3}/_{8}$ in. (10mm)

10 in. (250mm)

6 $^{3}/_{4}$ in. (170mm)

1 $^{1}/_{2}$ in. (40mm)

8 $^{1}/_{4}$ in. (210mm)

Begin by marking out your board as shown here.

1 Prepare your board as described on page 19. Once you have marked up and crosscut the board, rip the components to size. For stability, it is wise to make the tray from three pieces joined together. If they are correctly oriented, this helps to reduce the wood's tendency to cup and distort. Plane the edges smooth.

2 Lay the tray boards side by side on the bench, making sure that they are arranged with the growth rings on the end grain running in opposing directions on each board. This helps keep the tray surface flat. Mark the positions for the biscuit joints.

3 Cut the joints with a biscuit jointer.

4 Glue the boards together. For maximum strength, make sure that the biscuits are generously supplied with glue.

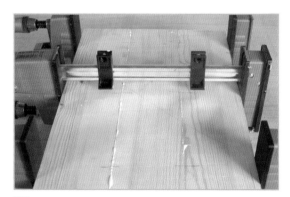

5 Clamp up securely and leave to cure.

6 Once the glue has set, remove the clamps and clean up the surface with a sander. If it is uneven, use a smoothing plane first.

PLATE RACK

There are many ways to store crockery in your kitchen. You can pile it all up in cupboards, you can display it on shelves—or you can use a plate rack. Here is a design for a plate rack that can be used as a freestanding unit or, if you remove the top and cut off the feet, attached underneath an existing wall cabinet.

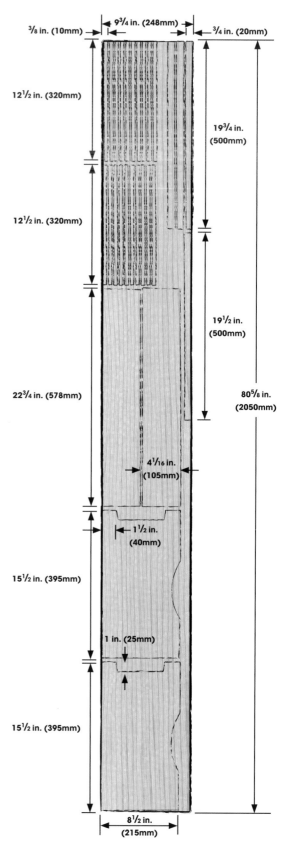

3/8 in. (10mm)

9 3/4 in. (248mm)

3/4 in. (20mm)

12 1/2 in. (320mm)

19 3/4 in. (500mm)

12 1/2 in. (320mm)

19 1/2 in. (500mm)

22 3/4 in. (578mm)

80 5/8 in. (2050mm)

4 1/16 in. (105mm)

1 1/2 in. (40mm)

15 1/2 in. (395mm)

1 in. (25mm)

15 1/2 in. (395mm)

8 1/2 in. (215mm)

Begin by marking out your board as shown here.

PLATE
RACK

● ● ● **YOU WILL NEED...**

- Tablesaw or handsaw

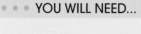

- Jigsaw or coping saw

- Sliding bevel

- Sander

- Pocket-hole jig

- Drill

- Screwdriver

- Clamps

1 Prepare your board as described on page 19. The rack obviously needs to fit your plates. This design is intended to fit 10½-in. (270-mm) -diameter plates. So take a plate and ensure that it will fit between the rails. Use two small offcuts from the rails to work out the spacing.

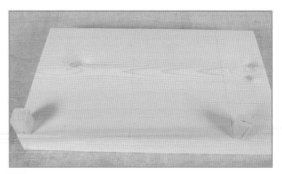

2 Mark out the positions of the rails according to the size of your plates.

3 The front edges of the rack have curved cutouts. A plate makes a good template.

4 Mark out the positions of the feet. Use a sliding bevel to mark the angle. The precise angle is not important, just choose one that looks right to you.

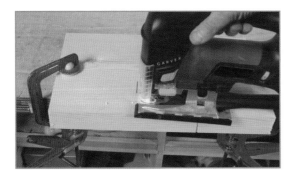

5 Clamp both side pieces together on the edge of the bench and cut out the front curve. A powered jigsaw is ideal for this (as here), or you could use a coping saw. Reclamp the boards and cut out the feet.

6 The rough edges of the saw cuts will need smoothing. With the sides still clamped together, sand the edges smooth. A drum sander is ideal, but the detail sander shown here does a pretty good job.

7 Cut the four rails to length. Use pocket screws to attach them to the sides. Clamp each rail into the jig and bore holes in both ends. Make sure that you bore them on the same face.

8 Screw the rails in position. A batten has been clamped onto the workbench and the side piece is held against it. This makes it much easier to align the rails with the edges when you are screwing them down.

9 Crosscut another length of board and then rip the uprights to size.

10 Lay out the uprights in the rack and work out the spacing, referring to your plate again. Ten were used here with a spacing of approximately 1⅜ in. (35mm) between them. The two sides are identical.

11 The ends of the uprights need to be notched to locate them on the rails properly. Mark the position of the notches with a pencil.

12 Now mark a line across the center of each upright to indicate the depth of the notch. Carefully cut out all the notches with a handsaw.

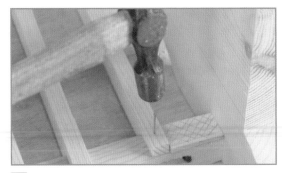

13 The uprights are attached to the rear of the cross rails with brads. Lay the uprights out on the rack and, rather than measuring the space between them, make a spacer piece. It will greatly speed up the nailing process.

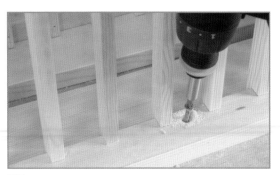

14 The top is made from a pair of boards separated by a 5/8-in. (16-mm) gap. These are attached with three screws through the top rails. Drill and countersink the holes, then screw into the boards.

15 The top boards also need to be attached on their inner edges to prevent them from bowing. Use a pocket screw in each corner. Wedge the drilling jig in place with an offcut pressed against it.

16 Insert the screws. If you do not have a small pocket-hole jig, the top can be held down with small metal brackets instead.

Your finished plate rack tray should look like this when complete.

BREAKFAST TRAY

How lovely it would be to have breakfast brought to you in bed every morning. Unfortunately, for most of us that is a rare luxury. On those special occasions when it does happen, though, it is important to have the right sort of breakfast tray. A normal tray is hard to balance in bed. The last thing you want is a coffee-soaked sheet or marmalade on your pillow. Here is a design for a tray with folding legs that will stand securely on the bed with legs extended. It can also be used with the legs folded.

BREAKFAST TRAY

● ● ● YOU WILL NEED...

- Tablesaw

- Jigsaw or coping saw

- Router table with roundover bit

- Biscuit jointer

- Biscuits

- Drill

- Screwdriver

- Web clamp

- Wood glue

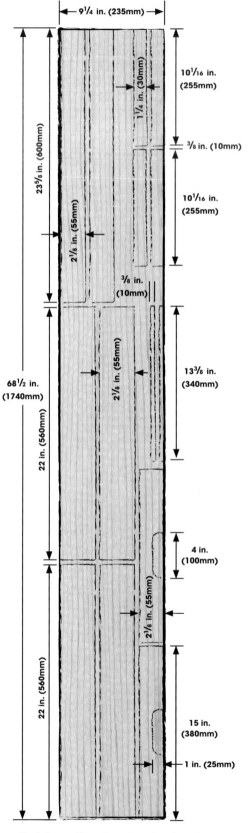

Begin by marking out your board as shown here.

1 Prepare your board as described on page 19. Mark out the components, then crosscut them to length.

2 Now rip the components to size.

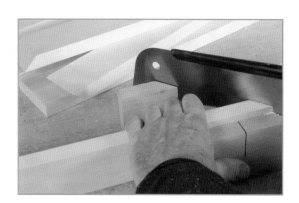

3 The tray frame has mitered joints on the corners. These can be cut using a tablesaw or miter saw. Alternatively, you could use a tenon saw or a pull saw (as here) and a miter box.

4 The two ends have handholds cut into their undersides. These should be about 4 in. (100mm) in length and 1 in. (25mm) high, so that your hands will fit comfortably. Mark them out with a pencil and try square.

5 Find a suitable template to mark the rounded corners. This can was ideal.

6 A jigsaw or coping saw can be used to cut out the handholds.

7 Clean up the curves with a small drum sander.

8 The edges of all the components need to be rounded over. The simplest way to do that is to use a bearing-guided roundover bit mounted in a router table. Remember not to round over the outer edges of the two outer boards of the tray, because they will be glued to the inside of the frame.

9 The boards will be biscuit-jointed into the frame. Roughly assemble the tray and line up the boards. Mark the position of the joints on the boards and the frame. You will need one biscuit on the end of each board and three biscuits along the outside edges of the outside boards.

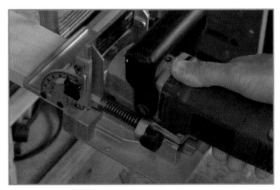

10 Set the jointer to cut your slots exactly in the center of the boards' thickness. Cut the end joints on all boards and the side joints on the outside boards.

11 Now reset the jointer fence so that it is ¼ in. (6mm) higher.

12 Cut the joints in the frame, running the fence against the top surface.

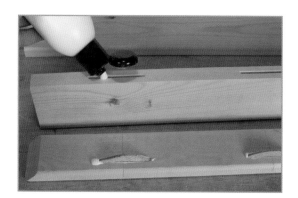

13 Glue up the joints and assemble the tray. Be careful not to use too much glue in the biscuit slots, because it will all squeeze out. Use enough to coat the biscuits thoroughly without too much overflow.

14 Clamp the assembly tight. A web clamp will do, but make sure that the corners are square by measuring the diagonals and ensuring that they are the same.

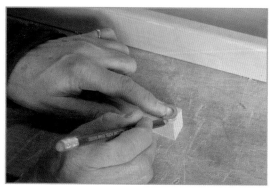

15 Once the tray is complete and the glue dry, attach the legs. Cut them to length and mark the ends for rounding over. A washer was used here.

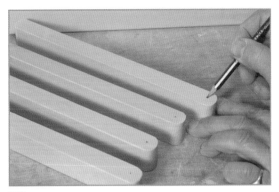

16 Once all the ends have been rounded over, mark the position of the pivot screw. This should be about ½ in. (12.5mm) from the end.

17 Drill a ⁵/₃₂-in. (4-mm) -diameter hole in each leg. A drill press is a good choice for this because it is important for the hole to be perpendicular.

18 Attach the legs to the inside of the frame about ¾ in. (19mm) in from the corner. Use a screw and cup washer, but do not overtighten it.

19 The legs need a crosspiece between them to provide additional stability. Drill pilot holes and countersink.

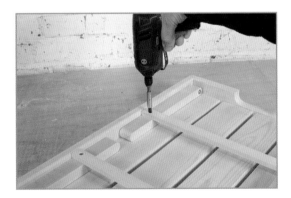

20 Fit the rails to the legs.

21 The completed tray folded.

● ● ● ONE-BOARD TIP:

When using screws to attach moving components such as folding legs, cup washers provide an efficient and decorative solution while preventing the screw head from marring the wood.

Your finished breakfast tray should look like this when complete.

FOLDING STOOL

Sometimes it is convenient to sit at your workbench, particularly when involved in intricate work. However, a stool takes up valuable floor space and can get in the way when you are not using it. Here is a simple design for a folding stool that can be stored in a corner—or even hung on the wall—when not needed.

FOLDING STOOL

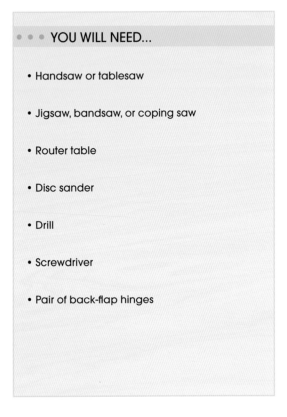

● ● ● YOU WILL NEED...

- Handsaw or tablesaw

- Jigsaw, bandsaw, or coping saw

- Router table

- Disc sander

- Drill

- Screwdriver

- Pair of back-flap hinges

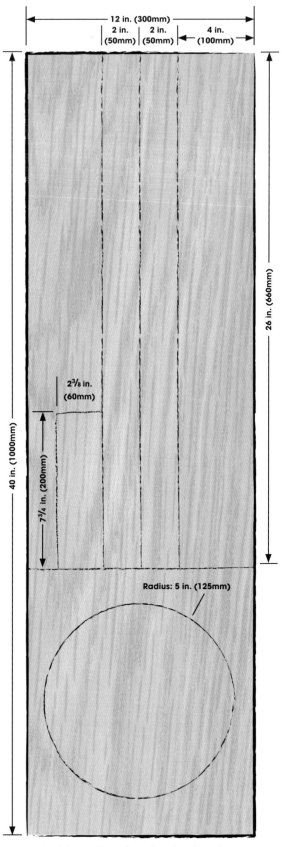

12 in. (300mm)

2 in. (50mm) 2 in. (50mm) 4 in. (100mm)

26 in. (660mm)

40 in. (1000mm)

$2\frac{3}{8}$ in. (60mm)

$7\frac{3}{4}$ in. (200mm)

Radius: 5 in. (125mm)

Begin by marking out your board as shown here.

1 Prepare your board as described on page 19. Mark out the board. Choose a sturdy one at least 1⅛ in. (28mm) thick.

2 Crosscut the end of the board to separate the seat component.

3 You can cut out the seat disc in a variety of ways. A powered jigsaw is ideal, but a fret saw or coping saw can also be used. A bandsaw is being used here with a simple homemade jig that pivots the workpiece around a nail to produce a perfect circle.

4 Turn the workpiece slowly—and be sure to use a narrow blade.

5 The cut-out seat.

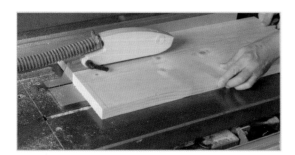

6 Cut the other components.

7 The edges of the seat need to be rounded over for comfort. A bearing-guided bit mounted in a router table is ideal for this.

8 Round over both sides of the seat.

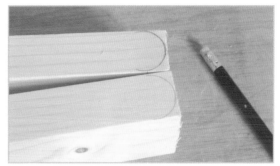

9 It looks good if you curve the tops of the two narrow legs, although this is not entirely necessary. If you do, mark out a curve with a suitable template.

10 Then shape the curve with a disc sander.

11 Position the three legs on the stool with the two narrow legs vertical and the large central leg horizontal. The vertical legs should be as near to the edge as possible without hanging over it.

12 Use a pair of back-flap hinges to attach the legs, keeping the central leg in position to protect the spacing. Run a countersink into each hole before inserting the screw. This ensures that the screw is centrally positioned in the hole.

13 Clamp all three legs together so that they are exactly lined up. Mark a point 6¾ in. (170mm) down from the top and drill a ³⁄₁₆-in. (5-mm) -diameter hole through each of the outer legs and into the central leg.

14 Use a no. 8- x 3¼-in. (80-mm) screw with a cup washer to secure each outer leg to the central leg. Do not overtighten it, as it must be free to swivel.

15 Attach a stop block to the underside to support the central leg. Angle its edge to match the leg's slope. To angle the leg bottom, stand the stool on the workbench, lay a pencil flat on the bench, and draw a line across the edge of the leg parallel to the bench. Trim the leg to this line.

16 The final job is to attach a brace between the two outside legs. Take a 2⅜-in. (60-mm) -wide length of board and reduce its thickness on the bandsaw to around ¾ in. (19mm). Trim the brace to length, which is the width of the three legs when laid flat.

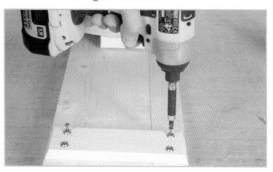

17 Attach the brace to the legs with no. 4 x 1¼-in. (30-mm) screws with cup washers.

Your finished stool should look like this when folded.

Your finished stool should look like this when complete.

WEATHERVANE

A weathervane adds the finishing touch to any building, from a garden workshop to a stately home. There are endless designs for weathervanes, from the mundane to the surreal. Here is a very straightforward one with an arrow-shaped vane.

Feel free to modify the design to suit your taste; however, there are two stipulations.

First, one end must have a larger surface area to catch the wind. Second, both ends must balance at the pivot point, otherwise the vane will not spin easily.

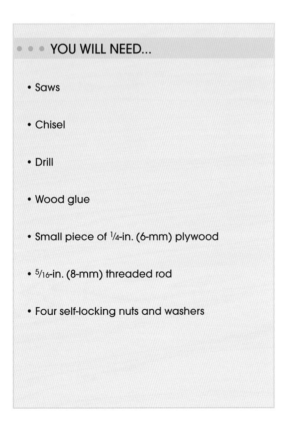

WEATHERVANE

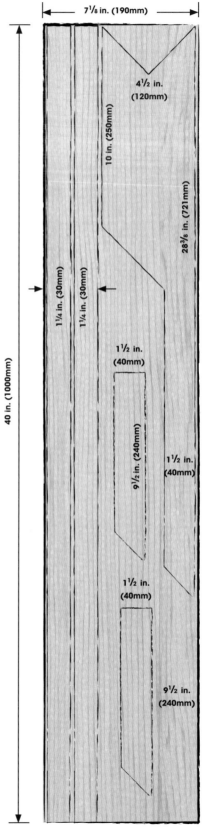

• • • YOU WILL NEED...

- Saws

- Chisel

- Drill

- Wood glue

- Small piece of ¼-in. (6-mm) plywood

- ⁵⁄₁₆-in. (8-mm) threaded rod

- Four self-locking nuts and washers

7¹⁄₈ in. (190mm)

4¹⁄₂ in. (120mm)

10 in. (250mm)

28³⁄₈ in. (721mm)

1¹⁄₄ in. (30mm)

1¹⁄₄ in. (30mm)

1¹⁄₂ in. (40mm)

9¹⁄₂ in. (240mm)

1¹⁄₂ in. (40mm)

1¹⁄₂ in. (40mm)

9¹⁄₂ in. (240mm)

40 in. (1000mm)

Begin by marking out your board as shown here.

1 Prepare your board as described on page 19. A tablesaw is good for ripping the straight components from the board.

2 A jigsaw will deal with the rest.

3 Cut the V in the rear of the vane.

4 The two side pieces are glued to the front end of the vane to balance it. Clamp them in place and allow time for the glue to dry.

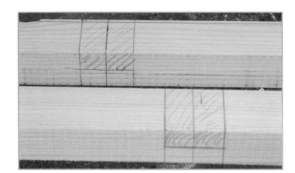

5 The two crossbars are joined with a simple half-lap joint. Mark this out by finding the center of each bar, then lay one across the other at a right angle. Mark the width of the upper bar on the lower bar and the width of the lower bar on the upper bar. Now measure down to half the thickness of the bar and mark a horizontal line.

6 Make a series of parallel cuts down to the marked line with a tenon or similar saw.

7 Remove the cut pieces with a chisel.

8 The completed joint, which can be glued in place.

9 Drill a 5/16-in. (8-mm) hole through the center of the joint for the threaded rod.

10 The next job is to make the indicators for the points of the compass. The simplest way is to print out the four letters from your computer. Try to find a simple font that will make the letters easy to cut out. They should be around 2 in. (50mm) high. Attach the prints to 1/4-in. (6-mm) plywood with spray-on adhesive.

11 A bandsaw is a good choice for cutting out the letters, although a jigsaw or fretsaw can also be used.

12 The completed letters. Note the additional 3/8-in. (10-mm) section on the base of each that will be used to mount them onto the crossbars.

13 Rout a ¼-in. (6-mm) wide groove at the end of each crossbar to take the letters. The simplest way to do this is with a router table, because it is difficult to balance a handheld router on such a narrow workpiece. Set the cutter depth to ⅜ in. (10mm).

14 Feed the 5/16-in. (8-mm) threaded rod through the crossbars and hold it in place with a pair of self-locking nuts and washers. Allow at least 12 in. (300mm) to extend below the crossbars so that you can use it to mount the completed weathervane.

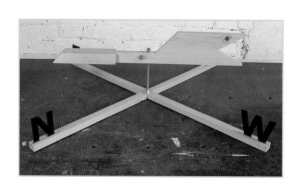

15 To finish, the vane is mounted on the top of the rod between a pair of self-locking nuts and washers. Before you bore the hole in the vane, find the balance point by laying a pencil on the bench and placing the vane upright on it so that it will balance. Bore the hole at this point. The letters are glued into the grooves on the crossbars close to the end. A coat of black paint will make them stand out.

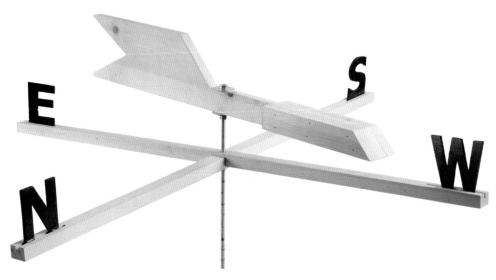

Your finished weathervane should look like this when complete.

TOOLBOX

Carrying tools around can be a real bore. You can buy all kinds of toolboxes and bags, but why not make your own? You can make it to suit your tools and customize it to fit any special accessories that you may have. This toolbox is based on a traditional design, but with a sliding tray that can be used for screws and small hardware.

TOOLBOX

• • • YOU WILL NEED...

- Saws

- Disc sander

- Drill

- Pocket-hole jig

- Screwdriver

- Wood glue

- ¾-in. (19-mm) -diameter dowel

- ¼-in. (6mm) plywood

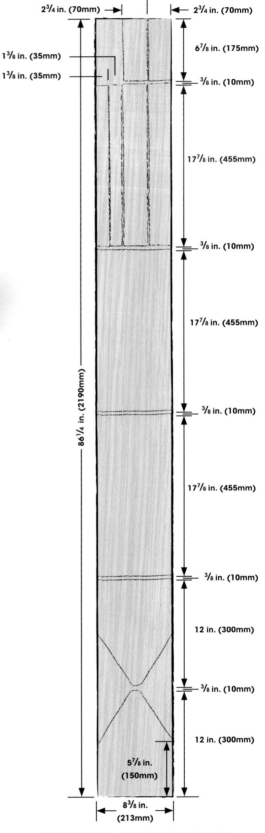

2¾ in. (70mm)

2¾ in. (70mm)

1⅜ in. (35mm)

1⅜ in. (35mm)

6⅞ in. (175mm)

⅜ in. (10mm)

17⅞ in. (455mm)

⅜ in. (10mm)

17⅞ in. (455mm)

⅜ in. (10mm)

86¼ in. (2190mm)

17⅞ in. (455mm)

⅜ in. (10mm)

12 in. (300mm)

⅜ in. (10mm)

12 in. (300mm)

5⅞ in. (150mm)

8⅜ in. (213mm)

Begin by marking out your board as shown here.

1 Prepare your board as described on page 19. When making identical pieces, it is much easier and neater if you can deal with them as one, so tape the cut out ends together and draw the shape on the top piece. Cut off the waste.

2 A disc sander is ideal for shaping the curved top. Note that the pieces are still taped together.

3 A hole needs to be bored for the dowel handle. Use a flat bit and, again, keep the pieces taped together. Remember to put a piece of scrap board underneath to protect the drill bit and leave a clean exit hole.

4 Cut the baseboard and the shelf to length. The joinery on this box is very simple. Pocket screws were used here, but biscuits or simply screwing through from the end into the base would be equally effective. Use a jig to drill the pocket hole.

5 Assemble the sides and the base.

6 To make the tray, rip four pieces to suit. Cut them to length and check the fit. The tray should be snug in the base, but no too tight—this is not a cabinet drawer, after all.

7 Use a piece of plywood for the base of the tray. This will sit in a groove cut with a straight bit into the inside faces of all four sides of the tray. Use a ¼-in. (6-mm) straight bit at a depth of ¼ in. (6mm), with the fence also set to ¼ in. (6mm) back.

8 Pocket screws were used to hold the tray together—here a double pocket jig was used for speed. Alternatively, you can just screw through the corners into the end grain.

9 Loosely assemble the tray and measure the inside length and the inside width. Add ½ in. (12mm) to both those dimensions and cut a piece of plywood to that size.

10 Assemble the tray.

11 The simplest way to fit the shelf and make sure the tray can slide in and out smoothly is to put a couple of spacers on top of the tray edges. A couple of pieces of thick sandpaper were used here. Lay the shelf in position.

12 Screw through the ends to hold the shelf in position. Attach a pair of side pieces to the shelf in the same way.

13 A piece of dowel is used for the handle. To ensure that it is a tight fit in the hole, cut a slot in each end, then make a pair of wedges.

14 Insert the dowel and hammer the wedges in place. Trim the ends and smooth them with a sander.

15 Use a scrap of wood to make a pair of rotating catches to keep the tray from falling out. Screw the catches in position on each side with a cup washer. Do not overtighten, because the catches must be free to swivel.

16 You can make special holders for your tools, like this grooved piece to hold a saw, which is simply glued in place.

17 You can also make holders for your drill bits by taking a small offcut and using each drill to bore its own storage hole. Then simply attach it to a convenient place on the box.

Your finished toolbox should look like this when complete.

DVD RACK

Here is a simple design for a rack to keep all your discs safely. It will accommodate both CD cases and DVD boxes. It is not difficult to make, and relies on accurate half-lap joints for stability. It is easy to expand if you need more space, and you could even fit a wood or glass shelf to the top to support your television.

DVD RACK

● ● ● **YOU WILL NEED...**

• Tablesaw or handsaw

• Chisel

• Biscuit jointer

• Biscuits

• Clamps

• Wood glue

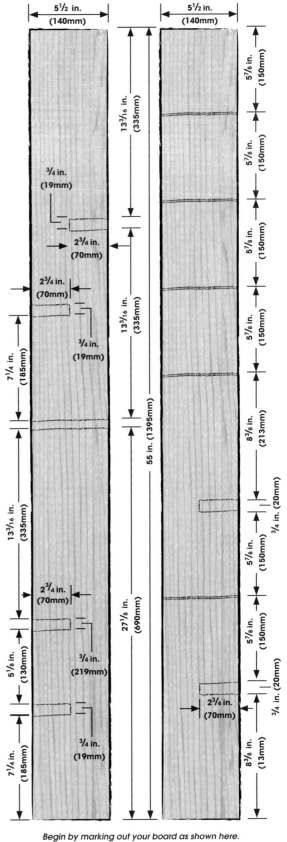

Begin by marking out your board as shown here.

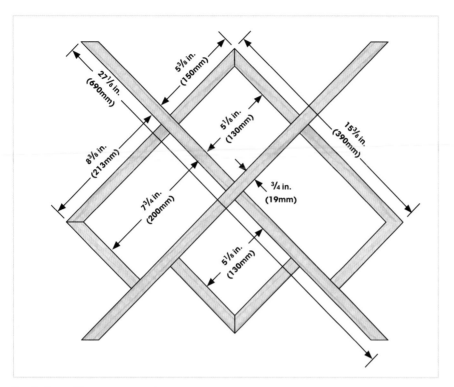

Front view with measurements

1 Prepare your board as described on page 19. The pieces all have mitered ends, and the easiest way to cut these is using a tablesaw (as here). However, you could also use a portable circular saw or a handsaw.

2 Once you have cut the boards to length, mark out the half-lap joints. Use an offcut of the board to ensure that they are exactly the right width.

3 The marked joints should look like this.

4 Again, the table saw is a good way to cut these joints; however, a handsaw is equally effective.

5 Work your way across the joint. Remember that the circular blade cuts at an angle, so leave a space in front of the marked line.

6 Pare out the waste with a chisel.

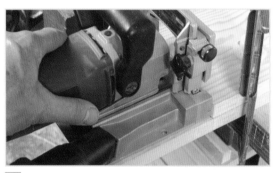

7 The simplest way to hold the mitered joints together is to use biscuits. Set your jointer fence to 45 degrees and cut a single slot in the mitered end of each board.

8 For the lowest section of the CD rack, you also need to cut joints in the board ends where they join the main frame. To do this, place the short board in position on the longer board. Mark a line across the long board at the rear of the short board. Now fold the short board back on the line and clamp it in position on the long board. Mark the center of the board and line up the jointer horizontally on it, using the base plate as the reference face. Cut a slot.

9 Then stand the jointer vertically on the board with its base against the slot that you have just cut and cut another slot in the long board.

10 The finished joint awaiting a biscuit.

11 To assemble the rack, start by making the biscuit joint and gluing the two short boards together. Clamp them in position if necessary.

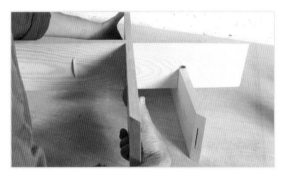

12 Next, apply glue to the half-lap joint on the two long boards and the half-lap joints on the shorter boards. Carefully slide the assembly together. A few gentle taps with a mallet may be needed.

13 Fit the two short end boards in position with biscuits and then take the final two boards and glue them together. Before the glue has cured, fit them onto the main frame with the two biscuit joints. Clamp in position if necessary.

Your finished DVD rack should look like this when complete.

SHOE RACK

Here is a design for a simple shoe rack. It takes up little space and will keep your shoes neatly out of the way. It is easy to make, but relies on tight joints to keep it secure. Take care when cutting them.

SHOE RACK

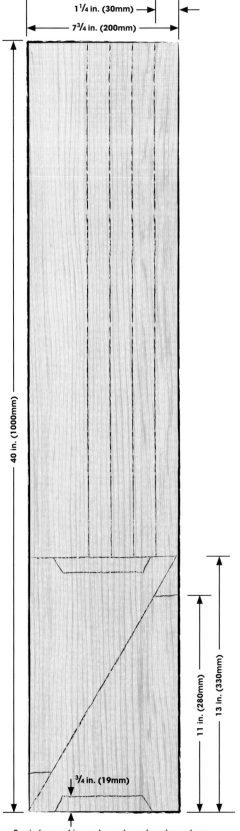

1¼ in. (30mm)

7¾ in. (200mm)

40 in. (1000mm)

11 in. (280mm)

13 in. (330mm)

¾ in. (19mm)

Begin by marking out your board as shown here.

1 Prepare your board as described on page 19. Mark up the board and then crosscut the end piece that makes up the two sides.

2 Cut the piece diagonally. This is an easy job for a bandsaw, but you could use a handsaw or jigsaw if you prefer.

3 Tape the two pieces together, then place them in a vise and plane both the sawn edges at the same time to make the pieces identical.

4 Now mark the cutout for the feet. Use a sliding bevel to mirror the slope of the front and make each foot 1¼ in. (30mm) wide. Join the two with a horizontal line ¾ in. (19mm) up from the base.

5 The tip of the triangular sides needs to be removed, so mark a horizontal line 10¼ in. (260mm) from the base and saw off the top.

6 Again, the bandsaw can be used to shape the feet, although a jigsaw or coping saw would also do the job.

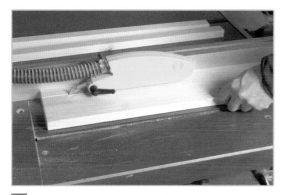

7 Rip the four rails. They are 1¼ in. (30mm) wide.

8 Now mark the joints. These are set ⅜ in. (10mm) in from the ends of the rails. The simplest method is to lay the rails flat on the bench and then stand the ends on them. Mark the joints with a pencil.

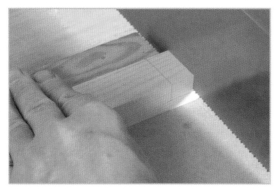

9 Use a tenon saw to cut down the sides of the joint. They should all be about ¹⁵/₃₂ in. (12mm) deep. Make a cut on each side of the joint and then several across the width.

10 Pare out the waste with a chisel.

11 Form a small chamfer around the exposed ends of the rails. A disc sander is the ideal tool for this, but you could use a block plane or even a chisel to achieve the same result.

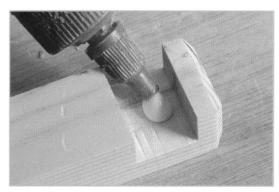

12 The joints alone should hold the rails in position tightly, so only a dab of glue is needed.

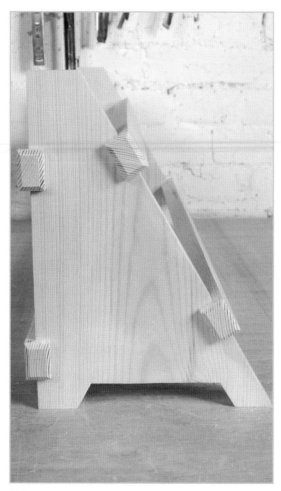

13 The precise position of the rails is not critical.

Your finished shoe rack should look like this when complete.

CLOTHES DRYING RACK

Drying clothes can be a chore. You can't rely on the weather, and the dryer costs a lot to run, so why not use a simple rack that can be placed next to a radiator or perhaps the kitchen range to provide economical and efficient drying. Here is a straightforward design that uses traditional joinery to make a useful and convenient unit that can be expanded to meet your needs. This design uses three identical frames.

CLOTHES DRYING RACK

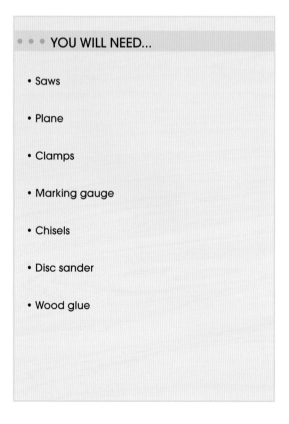

YOU WILL NEED...

- Saws

- Plane

- Clamps

- Marking gauge

- Chisels

- Disc sander

- Wood glue

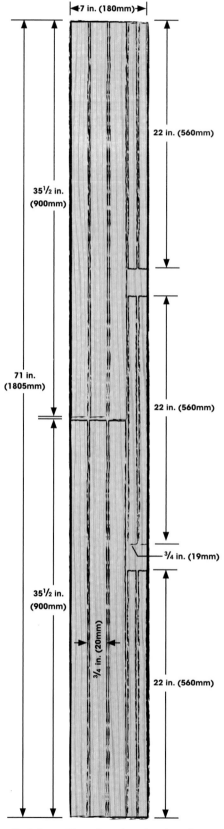

7 in. (180mm)

22 in. (560mm)

35½ in. (900mm)

71 in. (1805mm)

22 in. (560mm)

¾ in. (19mm)

35½ in. (900mm)

¾ in. (20mm)

22 in. (560mm)

Begin by marking out your board as shown here.

1 Prepare your board as described on page 19. Once you have crosscut and ripped the components, you will need to clean up the edges. Use a plane (as here) or a sander.

2 Take the six uprights and clamp them together. Use a try square to line them up and a 'C' or 'F' clamp to hold them in position.

3 The top rail should be located ¾ in. (19mm) from the top of the upright. Use a try square to mark the position.

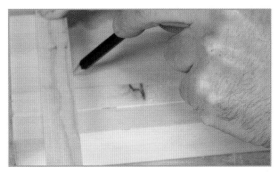

4 Use the rail to mark the exact width. Repeat for the lower rail, 19¾ in. (500mm) below the top.

5 The frames are held together using mortise and tenon joints. To mark the joints, you need to use a marking gauge. Set the width of the pins to match your chisel.

6 Mark the position of the joints on the uprights at ¾ in. (19mm) and 19¾ in. (500mm) from the top.

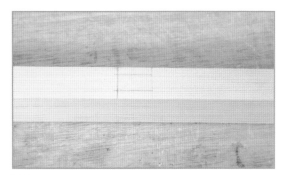

7 Use a pencil to mark the length of the joints, using one of the rails as a guide.

8 Mark the tenon width on the ends of the rails, again using the mortise gauge with the same settings as before.

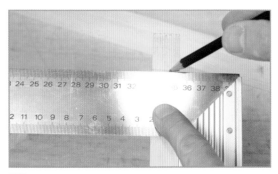

9 Mark the tenon shoulders with a try square. The tenons can go all the way through the stiles, but it is neater to make them stop short.

10 Use a chisel and mallet to pare away the waste in the uprights, working your way down to the base of the mortise in stages.

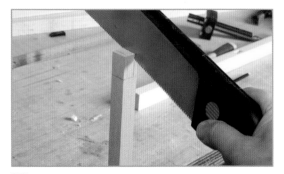

11 Stand the rails vertically in a vise and use a tenon saw or pull saw to saw down the tenon cheeks. Be careful to keep to the waste side of the marked line.

12 Cut the shoulders.

13 Test-fit the joints. You may need to shave a little off the tenon with a chisel to make it a snug fit.

14 The joint must fit tightly up to the shoulders.

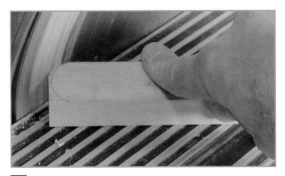

15 The tops of the uprights should be rounded over. Anything round and an appropriate size can be used to mark them. Then shape the curves with a disc sander.

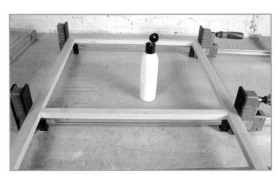

16 Dry-fit each of the frames and make sure that all the joints fit and that the frames are square. When you are satisfied, apply a little glue to the joints and then clamp up and leave to set.

17 To hinge the frames, you can fit metal hinges, make some fabric hinges, or use a pair of thick rubber bands like these.

Your finished clothes drying rack should look like this when complete.

WINE RACK

You never know when you might feel the need to celebrate, so it makes sense to keep a few good bottles of wine ready for that moment. You don't need to be a connoisseur to know that to keep wine at its best it should be stored horizontally so that the cork is kept moist. Here is a simple rack to hold eight bottles. There is some curved cutting to do, so you will need a narrow blade for your jigsaw or bandsaw. Alternatively, you could use a coping saw.

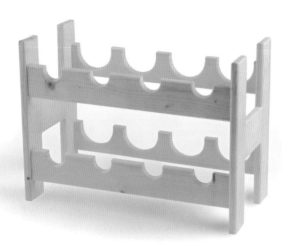

WINE RACK

• • • YOU WILL NEED...

- Compass

- Saws

- Drum sander

- Biscuit jointer

- No. 20 and No. 10 biscuits

- Router table and roundover bit

- Clamps

- Wood glue

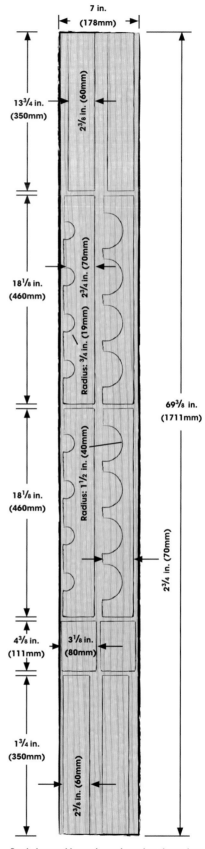

7 in.
(178mm)

13³/₄ in.
(350mm)

2³/₈ in. (60mm)

18¹/₈ in.
(460mm)

2³/₄ in. (70mm)

Radius: ³/₄ in. (19mm)

18¹/₈ in.
(460mm)

Radius: 1¹/₂ in. (40mm)

69³/₈ in.
(1711mm)

2³/₄ in. (70mm)

4³/₈ in.
(111mm)

3¹/₈ in.
(80mm)

1³/₄ in.
(350mm)

2³/₈ in. (60mm)

Begin by marking out your board as shown here.

1 Prepare your board as described on page 19. When marking out the components, make allowances if you are likely to be storing sparkling wine in sturdier bottles or bottles that are larger (or smaller) than standard sizes.

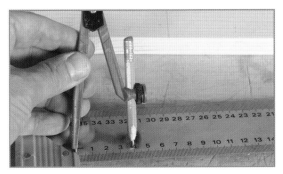

3 Now you need to use a compass to mark the curved supports for the bottles. For the two rear bars, set the radius to 1½ in. (40mm), and for the two front bars set the radius to ¾ in. (19mm).

2 Once you've cut out your components, take the four bars that support the bottles and lay them on the bench. On the two rear bars, mark a horizontal line ¾ in. (19mm) up from the bottom. On the front two, mark a horizontal line 1¾ in. (45mm) up from the bottom. Line up all the boards together perfectly square. Mark the center lines for the bottle cutouts. Work in from one end and mark one line in 2⅜ in. (60mm) and a second in an additional 4⁷⁄₁₆ in. (113mm). Repeat the procedure from the other end. Mark these lines across all four bars simultaneously.

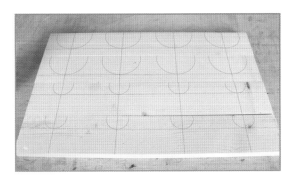

4 With the compass point on one of the vertical lines, draw a semicircle so that its circumference just touches the horizontal line where the two lines cross. Repeat for all four cutouts. Do the same for the front bars, using the smaller radius.

5 Clamp the bars to the workbench and carefully cut out the curves with a coping saw, bandsaw, or jigsaw (as here) fitted with a narrow blade.

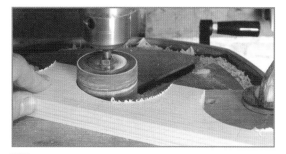

6 These will look a bit rough, so clean them up with a small drum sander mounted in a drill press or an electric drill.

7 The next job is to make the side frames. These are very simple and made in the form of an H. The horizontal bar is just biscuit-jointed into the two uprights. Arrange the components accurately and mark the positions of the two biscuits. Clamp the components to the workbench and cut the joint. Use No. 20 biscuits for this joint. Apply glue to the slots and assemble the two ends. Clamp up securely until the glue has dried.

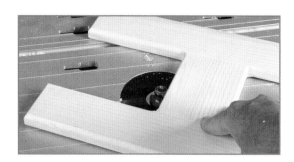

8 All the parts of the wine rack, including the support bars, should have their edges smoothed and rounded. The simplest way to do this is to use a bearing-guided roundover bit in a router table. Work along the curved edges and then turn the workpiece over and repeat on the other side. Round over the bottom edges and ends as well.

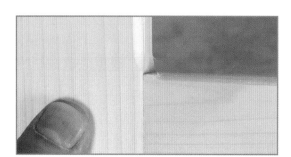

9 The cutter cannot get tight into corners, so there is always a small section that is left square. You can easily round this off with a little sandpaper.

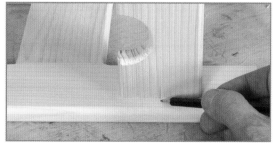

10 You are now ready to assemble the rack. You should use No. 10 biscuits for this joint. Start by marking a center line on all the bottle support rails. Then mark a line 2 in. (50mm) in from the ends of the side frames. Stand the support rails on the side frames with their bottom edges on the marked lines. Now mark off the position of the biscuit on the frame.

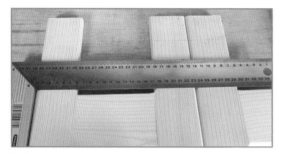

11 Use a try square to transfer the marks across to the second end frame.

12 Set your jointer for No. 10 biscuits and cut the slots in the ends of all the rails.

13 Because the rails need to be set back on the end frames, you need to reset the jointer fence so that it is ³⁄₁₆ in. (5mm) farther away from the blade. Then clamp the end frame in a vise with the inside face toward you and cut the slot for the biscuits using the lines you marked earlier. It is easier to see them if you extend them onto the edges of the uprights with a try square.

14 Once all the joints are cut, you are ready to start the assembly. However, before you do so, spend a little time cleaning up all the components with some sandpaper or a power sander to remove the pencil marks and any other blemishes.

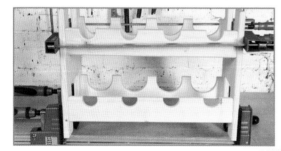

15 Assembly is straightforward. Apply a little glue to each of the biscuit slots, insert the biscuits and fit the rails. Make sure that all the rails are correctly set 2 in. (50mm) from the ends of the side frames. Use four bar clamps to hold the rack together while the glue cures.

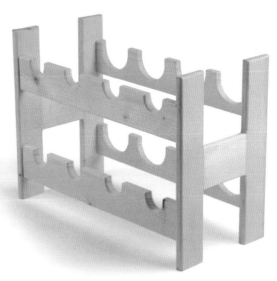

Your finished wine rack should look like this when complete.

STEP STOOL

There are times when we all need a little help to reach that top shelf or change a light bulb or, if you are very young, just to reach the sink! Here is a design for a little set of steps that would be ideal in the kitchen or perhaps in the bathroom for the younger family members. The joinery is all done with a pocket-hole jig, which makes it simple to assemble. However, you could use biscuit joints if you prefer.

STEP STOOL

● ● ● YOU WILL NEED...

- Saws

- Plane

- Clamps

- Power sander

- Drum sander

- Pocket-hole jig

- Screwdriver

- Wood glue

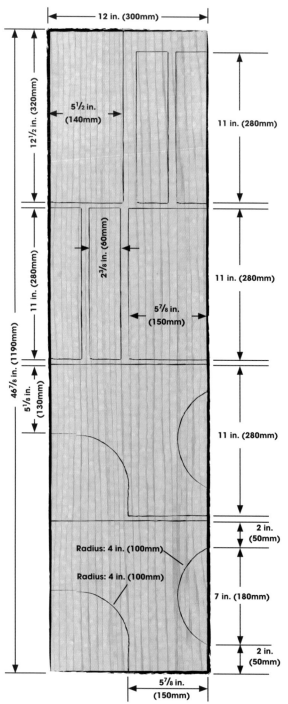

12 in. (300mm)

12½ in. (320mm)

11 in. (280mm)

5½ in. (140mm)

11 in. (280mm)

2⅜ in. (60mm)

11 in. (280mm)

5⅞ in. (150mm)

46⅞ in. (1190mm)

11 in. (280mm)

5⅛ in. (130mm)

11 in. (280mm)

2 in. (50mm)

Radius: 4 in. (100mm)

7 in. (180mm)

Radius: 4 in. (100mm)

2 in. (50mm)

5⅞ in. (150mm)

Begin by marking out your board as shown here.

1 Prepare your board as described on page 19. Mark out your board. Depending on your board, you may need to join several pieces to make up the sides. Divide the board into sensible widths to make an oversize panel that can be trimmed to size later. Alternatively, cut the sides out as a single piece.

2 First, crosscut the components to length, then rip them to width. Both these steps can be achieved with a handsaw if you do not have a tablesaw (as here).

3 Before jointing the boards to make up the sides, plane the edges so that they fit together neatly.

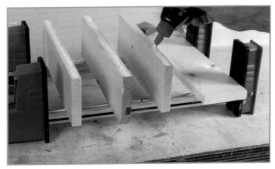

4 Apply a little glue to the boards. It is only necessary to apply glue to one edge of the joint.

5 Clamp the boards and allow the glue to cure, then clean up any roughness with a power sander.

6 Trim the panel to size, then mark two lines on the board, one vertical 5⅞ in. (150mm) in from the front edge and another horizontal 5⅞ in. (150mm) down from the top edge.

7 You could simply make a square cutout, but a curve looks better. A 7³⁄₄-in. (200-mm) -diameter saucepan lid was used here as a template to make the curve.

8 The lid was used again to mark the curve between the feet. Draw two vertical lines 2 in. (50mm) in from the front and back edges and position the lid between them to draw the curve.

9 Once both end panels are marked out ready for cutting, clamp the panel so that it overhangs the edge of the workbench. Use a jigsaw (as here) or coping saw to cut out the curves. If you have a long enough blade, you could clamp both sides together and cut them at the same time.

10 Use a small drum sander in a drill press or on an electric drill to smooth the curves and remove any saw marks. Then soften all the sharp edges with some sandpaper.

11 All the joints are pocket holes and are drilled using the simple jig shown. Make a pair of holes in the ends of each rail and three holes along the top of each rail.

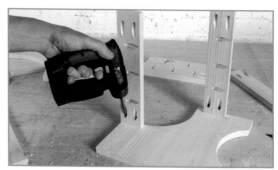

12 Lay one side panel on the bench and screw the rails into position.

13 Set the rails back a little from the edge of the side panel, as this produces a much neater appearance.

14 The completed frame.

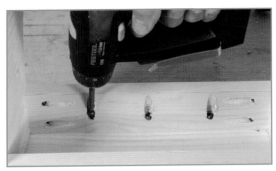

15 Invert the frame and screw the steps into position.

16 Carefully go over the whole piece with sandpaper, removing any blemishes or sharp edges so that it all feels smooth to the touch.

Your finished step stool should look like this when complete.

CORNER SHELVES

The corner of a room is often wasted space, but it is, in fact, an excellent place to hang shelves for display or storage. Corner shelving can look a little dull using the usual triangular shelves and rounded front edges, so here is a slightly more unusual design that is also versatile and decorative.